FRANCO-GERMAN RELATIONS
1871-1914

FRANCO-GERMAN RELATIONS
1871-1914

THE CREIGHTON LECTURE FOR 1923

BY

G. P. GOOCH, D.Litt.

NEW YORK / RUSSELL & RUSSELL

FIRST PUBLISHED IN 1922

REISSUED, 1967, BY RUSSELL & RUSSELL

A DIVISION OF ATHENEUM HOUSE, INC.

BY ARRANGEMENT WITH G. P. GOOCH

L. C. CATALOG CARD NO: 66−24694

PREFACE

THE task of the historian is interpretation, and the task of the politician is action. Yet the student may sometimes be of use in recalling the earlier phases and the deeper issues of problems which confront and confound the statesman. The record of Franco-German relations between the war of 1870 and the war of 1914 is not only one of tense dramatic interest, but it throws on the screen before our eyes the ambitions and activities, the groupings and the re-groupings, of the Powers. Within the limits of a single lecture it is impossible to do justice to so large a theme, or to make use of the mass of material which has poured from the archives of Paris and Berlin during the last few years. Its modest purpose is to attempt a bird's-eye view of a moving and passionate drama from the detached standpoint of an English observer who aspires to be, in the words of Talleyrand, 'a good European.'

G. P. G.

FRANCO-GERMAN
RELATIONS
1871-1914

THE War of 1914 was the outcome of three separate but
simultaneous antagonisms. The oldest was the quarrel
of France and Germany over Alsace and Lorraine.
Second in order of time was the competition of Russia
and Austria for hegemony in the Near East. The most
recent was the rivalry between Great Britain and Germany for the command of the seas. Of these problems
two have already been solved. The Anglo-German
feud ended at Scapa Flow. The Austro-Russian duel
terminated with the dissolution of the Hapsburg Empire.
The Franco-German conflict, on the other hand, has not
only survived but has been intensified by the Great War.
The Rhine Provinces, the Challenge Cup of Europe,
have changed hands once again ; but the Treaty of
Versailles possesses no more moral authority for Germans
than the Treaty of Frankfurt possessed for Frenchmen.
The quarrel of Paris and Berlin, which dominated and
poisoned the life of the Continent after 1870, dominates
and poisons it today.[1]

[1] The French side of the story is told in Bourgeois et Pagès, *Les Origines
et les Responsabilités de la Grande Guerre ;* Hanotaux, *Contemporary France ;*
Gontaut-Biron, *Mon Ambassade en Allemagne ;* Deschanel, *Gambetta ;* Mme.
Adam, *Souvenirs ;* E. Daudet, *La France et l'Allemagne ;* Freycinet, *Souvenirs ;*
Mévil, *De la Paix de Francfort à la Conférence d'Algésiras ;* Albin, *L'Allemagne
et la France*, 1885–1894 ; Caillaux, *Agadir ;* Tardieu, *Le Mystère d'Agadir ;*
Pinon, *France et Allemagne ;* Poincaré, *The Origins of the War.*

    The German version may be studied in *Die Grosse Politik der Europäischen
Kabinette ;* Bismarck, *Reflections and Reminiscences ;* Hohenlohe, *Memoirs ;*
Bülow, *Reden*, and *Imperial Germany ;* Reventlow, *Deutschlands Auswärtige
Politik ;* Rachfahl, *Deutschland und die Weltpolitik ;* Valentin, *Deutschlands*

I

The war of 1870, though welcomed by Bismarck, was begun by Louis Napoleon, and France, like other nations in similar circumstances, had to pay the debts of the Imperial gambler. But in the moment of victory the Iron Chancellor committed the greatest blunder of his life. After vetoing the annexation of Austrian territory in 1866 and thereby rendering possible a speedy reconciliation, he allowed the soldiers to have their way in 1871. 'After this war,' he declared on the morrow of Sedan, 'we must expect another aggression, not a durable peace, whatever conditions we impose. France will consider any peace a truce, and will try to avenge her defeat directly she feels strong enough, alone or with allies.' Outside France the annexation of Alsace and a portion of Lorraine was generally regarded as the natural punishment of the Power which had declared war and had been defeated. And where is the nation which, with bitter memories like those of the invasions of Louis XIV and Napoleon, would have returned empty-handed from a sanguinary struggle, and would have left in the possession of its defeated enemy rich territories which had formed part of its own vanished empire ? If France had won, she would doubtless have annexed the whole or part of the Rhineland. It is a crime to transfer masses of human beings from one allegiance to another against their will, but it is the common practice of conquerors. The peacemakers of 1919 have no title to cast stones at the peacemakers of 1871.

Yet Bismarck was partially aware of the unwisdom of the settlement which he was called upon to sanction. 'I did not want too many Frenchmen in my house,' he

Aussenpolitik; Aloys Schulte, *Frankreich und das linke Rheinufer;* Hammann, *Der missverstandene Bismarck.* Lord Newton, *Life of Lord Lyons;* Fuller, *Bismarck's Diplomacy at its Zenith;* and G. H. Stuart, *French Foreign Policy,* 1898–1914, are also useful. The most impartial study of the Rhine provinces is to be found in Coleman Phillipson, *Alsace-Lorraine.*

exclaimed. His plan, which received the weighty approval of the Grand Duke of Baden, was to content himself with Alsace, to dismantle Metz, and to exact a larger indemnity ; and it was a calamity for France, for Germany and for the world that it was not adopted. Perhaps he could not have got his way, for the Generals even resented leaving Belfort to France. But he never fought for his policy, and he deserves graver condemnation for the neglect of the *imponderabilia* than the soldiers whose horizon was bounded by strategical considerations. It is possible that Alsace, German in blood and language, might gradually have been reconciled by admission to the federal empire on equal terms with Baden and other South German states ; but Lorraine was bound to prove as indigestible as Posen. France never accepted the situation. The 36 deputies of the lost provinces unanimously protested against the cession, and 50,000 inhabitants left their homes within the year allowed for option. The story of Franco-German relations since 1871 is the record of France's endeavour to regain her lost territories and of Germany's attempt to retain them. The one remembered the aggression of 1870, the other the settlement of 1871 ; and the writers of schoolbooks took good care that the children should inherit the passions of their elders. There were pauses between the rounds, but the wrestlers never left the arena. Each of the protagonists sought and found allies, until almost the whole of Europe was involved in their implacable vendetta.

While Bismarck kept France in quarantine for twenty years by alliances or understandings with the other Powers, the French people manifested an admirable resilience and rebuilt the shattered fabric of their national life with extraordinary rapidity. In no responsible quarter was there a notion of challenging Germany to another conflict. ' The *revanche*,' writes René Pinon, ' was the natural and spontaneous reaction, the appeal to the future, arising from the abuse of force. It lived as a sacred ideal in the soul of the nation, but has never been

part of the Government programme.' She had to pay
her indemnity, terminate the occupation, frame a con-
stitution, restore her finances, and reform her army
before she could make fresh plans. ''Our policy is
peace,' declared Thiers ; 'a reorganised France will
always be necessary to Europe.' The gospel of work
was to restore to France her strength, her prosperity
and her self-respect.

The Monarchists possessed a majority in the Assem-
bly ; but they were divided, and the future lay with the
Republicans, whose hero, in peace as in war, was Gambetta. The first President could be none other than
the veteran Thiers ; but it was the hero of the National
Defence who represented France to herself and the world.
Perhaps in his own good time, it was whispered, in some
manner then undreamed of, he might be able to win
back the provinces. By tongue and pen he kept courage
and hope alive. He founded a journal, *La République
Française*, as ' a tribune from which the appeal for our
rights and our ravished provinces may be made before
Europe day by day. France is at the mercy of Germany.
We are in a state of latent war ; neither peace nor liberty
nor progress is possible.' France, he proclaimed in a
celebrated speech at St Quentin, must resume her rôle
in the world. ' Let us not speak of the foreigner, but
let him be ever in our thoughts. *Alors vous serez sur
le chemin de la revanche.*' ' Bismarck,' he wrote with
piercing foresight, ' has transformed a divided and
impotent Germany into a great, disciplined and powerful
empire. But the annexation of Alsace-Lorraine is the
death-germ of his work. In such an advanced civilisa-
tion moral conquest never follows material conquest.
Till they have repaired their error no one will lay down
his arms. The peace of the world will remain at the
mercy of an incident.'

Next to the great tribune a young poet named Paul
Déroulède was the most popular man in France. Enlist-
ing as a private in 1870 he had been wounded, taken
prisoner at Sedan, escaped, rejoined the French forces,

and fought to the end of the campaign. In 1872 he published a little volume entitled *Chants du soldat,* which, like the *Nouveaux Chants* three years later, were hailed with gratitude and enthusiasm throughout the country, and hummed by the young conscripts at their work as Körner's lyrics had been sung in Germany sixty years earlier. His songs, with their simple vocabulary and obvious rhymes, printed in pocket editions for a few sous and in illustrated editions for a few francs, sold by scores of thousands and fostered the moral convalescence of France. The opening poem of the first volume was entitled

VIVE LA FRANCE

Oui, Français, c'est un sang vivace que le vôtre !
Les tombes de vos fils sont pleines de héros.
Mais, sur le sol sanglant où le vainqueur se vautre,
Tous vos fils, O Français, ne sont pas aux tombeaux.

Et la revanche doit venir, lente peut-être,
Mais en tout cas fatale, et terrible à coup sûr ;
La haine est déjà née, et la force va naître :
C'est au faucheur à voir si le champ n'est pas mûr.'

Perhaps the most popular of the series was the poem to the *poilu.*

Dans la France, que tout divise,
Quel Français a pris pour devise
Chacun pour tous, tous pour l'État ?
Le Soldat.

Dans nos heures d'indifférence,
Qui garde au cœur une espérance
Que tout heurte et que rien n'abat ?
Le Soldat.

Qui fait le guet quand tout sommeille ?
Quand tout est en péril, qui veille ?
Qui souffre, qui meurt, qui combat ?
Le Soldat

O rôle immense ！ O tâche sainte ！
Marchant sans cris, tombant sans plainte,
Qui travaille à notre rachat ?
Le Soldat.

Et sur la tombe obscure et fière,
Pour récompense et pour prière,
Que voudrait-il que l'on gravât ?
Un Soldat.

The few Frenchmen who accepted the situation were regarded with anger and contempt. When the Alsatian Scheurer-Kestner, then a young man, visited Grévy, the first President of the Chamber, he received an unwelcome homily. ' " My children, it is grievous to have lost one's country ; but the régime which weighed so long on France could only leave disaster behind. I know you are for war. I tell you, who voted against the peace,— France must not think of war. She must accept the *fait accompli*, she must renounce Alsace." The tears rolled down our cheeks. The President took us by the hand and added, " Do not believe the madmen who tell you the contrary, and who are the cause of our troubles being increased by a hopeless struggle." Resenting the reference to Gambetta we went away broken-hearted, as if an evil genius had taken from us the remainder of our courage. That day I judged Grévy. Since then I have only had official relations with him.' [1] Grévy, however, never ventured to say in public what he said in private, and no French Minister of the Third Republic ever dared or desired to accept the Treaty of Frankfurt.

Bismarck was under no illusion as to the sentiments of his vanquished foe. When the French Chargé, in his first interview in August, 1871, expressed his confidence that relations would improve, the Chancellor replied that he was glad to hear such language but could not believe that France sincerely desired peace. ' I do not think you wish to break the truce now. You will pay the first two milliards, but in 1874, when the other

[1] *Souvenirs de Jeunesse*, pp. 262–4.

three are due, you will fight us.' ' France,' added the
Chargé in reporting the conversation, ' is recovering too
quickly. He thought that he had finished with her for
twenty years at least, and he is becoming alarmed.'
When Gontaut-Biron took up his duties at Berlin early
in 1872 he received a cordial welcome from the Emperor
and Empress ; but the Chancellor, though at first
polite, took no pains to hide his sleepless suspicion.
The despatches of the first Ambassador of the Republic
depict a relationship of tension and protests, explanations and menaces, in which each party suspected or
pretended to suspect the other of designs to renew the
struggle.

Arnim's despatches from Paris were as pessimistic as
those of Gontaut-Biron from Berlin. Thiers, he reported
on May 6, 1872, desired a long peace, since France
was not in a position to wage a new war. Later when
France had recovered her strength, declared the President, she would naturally seek compensation for her
losses ; and if Germany were ever in difficulties with
other Powers she would find her chance, by bartering
her aid if not by war. ' There can be no doubt,' wrote
the German Ambassador on October 3, 1872, ' that of the
38 million Frenchmen not one hundred thousand regard
the present frontier as permanent. The instinct for
revenge, indeed, is so deep that they are not conscious
enough of the unfavourable diplomatic and military
situation to prevent them one day being suddenly carried
away by their passions. The German Empire can no
more co-exist with the France of today than Rome with
Carthage.' Bismarck replied to these gloomy vaticina-
tions (December 20) that France was not dangerous
without allies, that the Republic was much less likely
to find friends than a monarchy, and therefore that the
French royalists should not be supported. ' The frankness with which hatred of Germany is proclaimed and
encouraged by all parties,' he added on February 2,
1873, ' leaves us in no doubt that any Government will
regard the *Revanche* as its principal task. The only

question is how long the French will need to organise
their army or their alliances before they think they can
resume the struggle.   Directly that moment arrives the
Government will be compelled to declare war on us.'
The danger appeared to be increased by the fall of
Thiers and the substitution of Marshal MacMahon,
with the Duc de Broglie as Foreign Minister, which
the Chancellor interpreted as a step towards a royalist
restoration.   When Arnim was recalled in 1874 for
encouraging the royalists, Bismarck gave Hohenlohe,
his successor, the maxim for his guidance that France
must not obtain sufficient strength at home or considera-
tion abroad to secure allies.

   The unexpectedly rapid recovery of France, the pay-
ment of the indemnity in two years instead of four, the
increase of the army, and the persistent refusal of public
opinion to accept the Treaty of Frankfurt as anything
more than a truce angered Bismarck and alarmed the
military authorities in Germany.   In 1873 several of
the French Bishops indulged in violent comments on
the May Laws and the Kulturkampf.   The irascible
Chancellor decided that a sharp warning was needed.   It
was not enough that the Bishops were ordered by the
French Government to abstain from attacks, he declared
to the French Ambassador ;   they must be punished.
' It is a question of our security.   Your Bishops foment
revolt in the empire, and that we cannot stand.   If you
allow these proceedings to continue, you will make war
inevitable ;   and we shall begin it before the clerical
party gains power and declares war.   That is why
I dislike your projects of restoring the monarchy.   I
mistrust the influence which your clericals would have
on the Comte de Chambord.'   The threat was publicly
repeated in the *Norddeutsche Allgemeine Zeitung*, which
declared that from the moment France identified herself
with Rome she would become the enemy of Germany,
and that peace could not subsist with a France subject
to the Vatican.   ' If France supports the Catholics in
Germany,' he added ominously, ' I shall not wait till

she is ready, as she will be in two years, but I shall seize a favourable opportunity.' Moltke spoke ominously of approaching events, and Bülow, the Foreign Secretary, warned the Ambassador that the repetition of episcopal imprudences might lead to very grave complications. The Bishops were muzzled though not punished, and the rest of 1874 passed without incident, except that in the first general election fourteen out of fifteen members from the Reichsland protested against the annexation, demanded a plebiscite and left the Reichstag. The Chancellor had no desire to attack France, but he did not intend to allow another attack on Germany. 'We wish to keep the peace,' he observed in 1874 to Hohenlohe ; ' but if the French so order their preparations that in five years they will be ready and determined to strike, then in three years we shall begin war.' Since the Treaty of Frankfurt imposed no limit on armaments, Bismarck could only proceed by warnings and threats ; and in 1875 the nerves of Europe received a formidable shock.[1]

At the end of February Bismarck was informed that France was ordering a large number of cavalry horses in Germany, and, after forbidding their export, he wrote for explanations to Hohenlohe. The Ambassador replied that France had no present intention of war, but that all parties hoped to reconquer the provinces when she found allies. A few days later, on March 12, the French Chamber, outstripping the proposals of the Government, increased the battalions in a regiment from three to four. The German Staff calculated that the increase would be 144,000, which would make the French army larger than their own. ' This means an attack very shortly,' observed Moltke to the Belgian Minister ; ' we must not wait till they are ready.' Opinion was genuinely alarmed, and on April 5 the

---

[1] J. V. Fuller, ' The War-Scare of 1875,' *American Historical Review*, Jan. 1919, states the case against Bismarck. K. Herzfeld, *Die deutsch-französische Kriegsgefahr von 1875*, and Rachfahl, *Deutschland und die Weltpolitik*, i. 45–76, defend him.

Kölnische Zeitung expressed its fear of a Franco-Austrian alliance with the backing of the Pope and a clerical Monarchy in France. On April 9 the *Post* published an article headed 'Is War in sight?' which created the most dangerous crisis since 1871. War, it declared, was in sight, but it was still possible that the clouds might disperse. It was widely believed that the article was inspired by the Chancellor ; but the supposition was unfounded, for it was written by Rössler on his own responsibility. Bismarck told Hohenlohe that he was surprised by the article, but he welcomed it as calculated to awaken Germany to the danger and to frighten France ; and on April 11 the *Norddeutsche Allgemeine Zeitung* declared that, though the fears of the *Post* in regard to Austria and Italy were groundless, its anxieties about French armaments were correct. 'The burden is too heavy even for the richest country to bear for long,' added the semi-official organ ; 'they can only be preparations for the object which no clear eye can fail to see.'

On April 15 Gontaut-Biron, who had been away from Berlin, returned to his post and explained to the Foreign Minister that the horses had not been ordered by the War Office, that the simultaneous reduction of the size of the battalion would reduce the increase of the army to about 30,000 men, and that there was no thought of attack. Bülow appeared to be satisfied ; and the same evening the Kaiser, meeting the French Military Attaché at a reception, observed, 'People have been trying to make us quarrel, but the danger is over.'

The danger was not over, for Gontaut-Biron learned from friends that Bismarck was not yet pacified ; and on April 21, at a dinner at the British Embassy, he heard from the lips of Radowitz, a prominent diplomatist, words which filled him with terror. When he complained of the press campaign and spoke of the pacific intentions of France, Radowitz replied, 'Can you answer for the future ? France is bent on revenge. Why then should we wait till she is strong and has found allies ? ' Radowitz's own report of this conversation suggests that he was merely explaining the ideas which found utterance in the German press.[1] The Ambassador, however, feared that he was expressing the views of the Chancellor, and that a preventive war might be launched at any moment. His report alarmed Decazes, the Foreign Minister, who instantly forwarded a copy to the representatives of France abroad, with instructions to bring it to the notice of the Governments. At the same time he ordered the Ambassador at Petrograd to appeal for a public promise to draw the sword in the event of a German attack. The Tsar had already told Le Flô that there was no danger, and that if there were to be, he would tell France himself. He now replied, ' I shall not draw the sword, nor will you.' He added that he was shortly to visit Berlin. Meanwhile Decazes explained to Hohenlohe that France did not want war and could not wage it. If Germany invaded French territory, he added, she would withdraw her troops without fighting.

On May 5 the French Foreign Minister received a fresh shock, when Hohenlohe informed him of a despatch just received from the Wilhelmstrasse. The German Government, it declared, was not entirely convinced of the inoffensive character of French armaments, and the General Staff considered war as the ultimate object of the recent military measures. Decazes, fearing that the next step might be a demand for the reduction of the army, informed Blowitz of the situation, and on May 6 a despatch from its Paris correspondent entitled ' A French Scare ' appeared in the *Times*, revealing the threats and arguing that Russia alone could prevent a conflict. The article aroused consternation throughout Europe ; but on the previous day Schuvaloff, the Russian Ambassador in London, had passed through Berlin and explained to the Kaiser and Bismarck his master's attitude. Lord Derby instructed the British Ambassador at Berlin energetically to support Russian

[1] *Die Grosse Politik*, i. 275-7.

representations, and Andrassy assured Russia of the approval of Austria.   Annoyed at what he called British credulity Bismarck informed the British Ambassador that the project of a German attack was a legend ; and when the Tsar and Gortchakoff reached Berlin on May 10 they were met with peaceful assurances.   The six weeks' crisis was over.   The French President wrote to thank the Tsar for his timely aid, and Decazes spoke cheerfully of the resurrection of Europe.

That a preventive war was advocated by the army chiefs in Germany, and that cool observers like Lord Derby believed in the danger, is beyond dispute ; but we cannot be quite certain what was in Bismarck's mind. The statement in his *Reflections* that ' the myth of a German attack ' was a conspiracy against him engineered by Gontaut-Biron is ridiculous ; but there is no ground for the belief that he had resolved to unleash the dogs of war and was only restrained by the veto of Russia. ' Bismarck,' observed the Duc Decazes, ' wants us to believe that he wishes for war, but he does not wish for it himself.'   Though he did not share the views of Moltke, he desired France to know that Germany was watching her very closely, and that she would be wise to abstain from measures which might seem to point towards a renewal of the struggle.   But the policy of intimidation may easily lead to war without intending it. His resentment against Gortchakoff and Derby, and his fruitless request for the recall of Gontaut-Biron shewed that something had gone awry ; and he was conscious that he had partially forfeited the confidence in him which the friends of peace throughout Europe had begun to entertain.

The conflagration in the Balkans which began soon after the war-scare claimed Bismarck's attention for the next three years and thereby diminished the tension in the West.   He continued to dread the royalist movement in France, and feared that MacMahon's clerical sympathies might lead him to attempt a *coup*.   ' If the French Government can permanently free itself from clericalism,' he wrote to Hohenlohe in 1876, 'good relations would be easy and there would be less chance of the *revanche*.' He declined an invitation to take part in the exhibition planned for 1878, despite the desire of the Kaiser and the Crown Prince to accept it. His fears seemed to be confirmed by the anti-Republican demonstration of May 16, 1877, when the President dismissed the Ministry of Jules Simon and appointed the Royalist leader the Duc de Broglie ; and he observed that the France which stood behind MacMahon would not be able to avoid war.

II

A welcome *détente* began with the elections of December, 1877, which removed the fear of a monarchical restoration. The recall of Gontaut-Biron, with whom the Chancellor had hardly been on speaking terms since the crisis of 1875, was hailed by him as an olive-branch, though his departure brought tears to the eyes of the aged Emperor. The appointment of the Comte de St Vallier, who had established excellent relations with Manteuffel during the occupation, confirmed the favourable impression of the Dufaure Ministry and of Waddington, the new Foreign Secretary. On February 4, 1878, the Ambassador reported that the members of the Bundesrath saw in his appointment ' a new era,' and the Chancellor shewed himself ' particularly amiable ' in their first interview. An invitation to take part in the Congress of Berlin was accepted, and Bismarck went so far as to offer Waddington the Presidency. Even in Alsace-Lorraine there was a slight temporary *détente*. In the election of 1877 five Autonomists were returned, and in 1879 a Statthalter was appointed ; but when in 1881 Manteuffel invited loyal recognition of the annexation, the Autonomists disappeared and ' resolute government ' was again the order of the day. It was a sharp reminder of the inexorable limits of the *détente*.
When Waddington learned during the Congress of

Berlin that Great Britain had secured the occupation of Cyprus from Turkey, he told Beaconsfield that he must withdraw ; but Salisbury was ready with a *solatium*. ' You cannot leave Carthage in the hands of barbarians. Do what you like there.' The advice was supported by Bismarck, and on his return Waddington secured from Salisbury a written assurance of *désinteressement* in Tunis. No action was taken at the moment ; but the conversations at Berlin opened a new chapter in Franco-German relations. In January, 1879, Bismarck invited St Vallier to Friedrichsruh, where he urged the seizure of Tunis. ' I think that the pear is ripe and that it is time for you to gather it. I do not know if it tempts you, but I must repeat what I said last year to M. Waddington. My desire is to give you pledges of good-will in matters which concern you and where German interests do not collide with yours. It is only fair, for I appreciate the efforts which he and you have made to restore confidence between our two countries. Neither the Emperor nor I want another war on our hands. I believe that the French people need some satisfaction for their *amour-propre*, and I sincerely desire to see them obtain what they want in the Mediterranean, their natural sphere of expansion. The more success they find in that sphere the less will they be moved to assert their grievances against us.' When the Ambassador observed that he should report these words textually, the Chancellor replied that he would put them in writing if requested. It has often been argued that the object of this suggestion to France to take Tunis was to drive a wedge between France and Italy. He may have foreseen such a result ; but he could not know in advance that France would seize the country without consulting or compensating her rival, and the wisdom of finding an outlet for the reviving energies of France outside Europe was so obvious that we need seek no other deciding motive.

The sun continued to shine for several years. When the Powers met at Madrid in 1880 to discuss problems of jurisdiction in Morocco, Bismarck instructed the

German representative to follow the lead of his French colleague ; and when in 1881 France proceeded to establish a Protectorate over Tunis by force of arms, he afforded the moral support which had been promised and for which he received an expression of cordial gratitude from Jules Ferry. It was at this moment (July, 1881) that Hohenlohe was instructed to convey to the Foreign Minister the Chancellor's hope that France would one day realise that German friendship was of more value than a million inhabitants of Alsace and Lorraine. The message was received by Barthélemy St Hilaire, Ferry's Foreign Minister, with a smile but without comment. 'We wish for the friendship of Germany, not her protection,' he wrote to St Vallier. The statesmen of France naturally preferred smiles to frowns, but they were well aware that there were limits to the Chancellor's indulgence. 'Russia is inclined to a *rapprochement*,' explained Waddington to Freycinet in handing over the reins in 1879, 'but Bismarck has his eye on us. The menace of an alliance might decide him to open hostilities.' The velvet glove scarcely concealed the iron hand.

The *détente* which began in 1877 was fully approved by the greatest of French citizens. Gambetta's hunger for the recovery of the provinces remained, but after the crisis of 1875 the possibility of winning them by negotiation occupied his thoughts. He was no longer the *fou furieux* he had seemed to Thiers. We can trace the evolution of his thought in his correspondence with Ranc and in the sparkling memoirs of his Egeria, Mme Adam. 'If by diplomacy we can avoid or at least postpone the conflict,' he wrote in September, 1875, 'should we not try it ? But how ? Our colonies. Which is the best, to keep our distant possessions or our future generations ? Let us face this cruel dilemma,— the lives of young France or portions of our colonial territory. Ought we not to profit by the taste of Germany for colonies ? We have what they want. Is that not our chance ? ' The rumour that Bismarck was about to visit Paris for political conversations in December, 1875, filled him with excitement. 'Must I stand aloof? Is it really my duty as a Frenchman? You know the dreams of a colonial future for his people, and his country is strong, perhaps invincible. Should we not avoid the noble but fruitless sacrifice of our young men whose death would enfeeble France for ever?' When Bismarck announced in 1878 that a Congress would meet at Berlin, Gambetta, after brief hesitation, favoured participation. 'We must profit by the rival ambitions to declare our legitimate demands and to create an agreement.' His readiness to meet the Chancellor had now grown into eagerness. At the end of 1877 Count Henckel von Donnersmarck, returning to Paris where he had lived under the Second Empire, wrote to Bismarck, 'I guarantee to bring Gambetta to Varzin on a public or a private visit, whichever you prefer. He will propose to you a *rapprochement* and a collaboration with France.' The Chancellor evaded a reply; but when the proposal was renewed in April, 1878, he accepted it, and a *rendez-vous* was arranged for April 30 at Berlin. At the last moment, however, Gambetta drew back. 'Man proposes, Parliament disposes,' he wrote to Henckel on April 18. 'When I readily accepted yesterday I did not allow for the unexpected. The questions relating to the Ministry of War have become increasingly important. I cannot abandon my post. So I must postpone the execution of the plan.'

The state of business was a pretext, for at the last moment Gambetta shirked the interview. It could only have led to disappointment, for, according to Blowitz, Bismarck told Holstein that he would have made it a condition that the provinces should not be mentioned. The faithful Spuller, who detested the notion of a *rapprochement*, warned his beloved leader to be prudent, and the *pourparlers* were never resumed, though Gambetta continued his visits to Germany and to the end Bismarck desired to meet him. Gambetta persevered in the new path, and a common friend encouraged him to hope for a change when the Crown Prince should come to the throne. Some of his friends turned their backs on the lost leader, who had secretly abandoned the *revanche*. 'You follow your sentiments, I my reason,' he remarked to Madame Adam in 1878, 'let each of us go his own way.' The *revanche* was merely a means to an end,—the recovery of the provinces, and Gambetta had come to believe that it might ultimately be secured without a war, perhaps by an alliance with England and Russia. He continued to make speeches which suggested that another conflict was inevitable, and in Germany it was believed that his accession to power might be the signal for the attack. ' *Les grandes réparations*,' he declared in his celebrated speech at Cherbourg in 1880, ' *peuvent sortir du droit*. We or our children can hope for them, for the future is open to us all. It has been said that we have a passionate cult for the army. It is not the spirit of war which animates this cult; it is the necessity, after seeing France fall so low, to raise her up so that she resumes her place in the world. If our hearts beat, it is for this goal, not for an ideal of blood ; it is that what is left of France may remain entire ; it is that we may count on the future. There is on earth an immanent justice which comes at its appointed time.' Freycinet, to whom some of the Ambassadors complained, assured them that the speech was pacific in intention ; but his critics cried, ' *Gambetta, c'est la guerre*,' and Bismarck exclaimed, ' Gambetta in power would act on the nerves like a man beating a drum in a sick-room.' A year later, at Menilmontant, he made his pacific attitude clear beyond controversy. ' France intends to win for herself such power and such prestige that in the end, by force of patience, she will receive the reward of wise and good conduct. If she is vigilant and prudent, taking her share in international affairs but eschewing conspiracy and aggression, I think and hope I shall see the day when, through the majesty of right, truth and justice, we shall regain our lost brothers.'

The Republican triumph of 1877 made Gambetta's accession to power a mere matter of time ; and when Grévy succeeded MacMahon as President in 1879, it was felt that the hour was nigh. Grévy, however, whether owing to jealousy or to fear of foreign complications, postponed the summons, and it was not till the summer of 1881 that even the President confessed that the next Ministry must be formed by the great Republican leader. The Kaiser was a little apprehensive, and St Vallier attempted to remove his fears by describing a recent conversation with Grévy. ' So long as I hold my post,' declared the President, ' I will never allow France to launch an attack. I shall know how to pursue and make all the Ministers pursue a policy of peace. In home affairs I shall not intervene, but I will never compromise on the maintenance of good relations. Germany can count on me and trust my word.' When *Le Grand Ministère* was at last formed in December, 1881, Gambetta asked St Vallier to report the effect. The Ambassador replied that the Kaiser was apprehensive and Bismarck suspicious ; but official relations remained friendly. The Chancellor informed St. Vallier and Hohenlohe assured the Quai d'Orsay, that the formation of the Gambetta Cabinet would in no way diminish the friendliness of Berlin. *Le Grand Ministère*, however, which was expected to make history, only lasted two months, and in less than a year the great patriot died in his forty-fifth year. That he had ceased to desire a war of revenge was known only to his intimate friends.

The *rapprochement* inaugurated by Waddington and approved by Gambetta was confirmed by Freycinet and Jules Ferry. At no time since 1870 had the wires between Paris and Berlin worked so smoothly as during the second Ministry of Ferry, which lasted from 1883 to 1885. The chief architect of the new French colonial empire, himself a Lorrainer, lamented the defeat of 1870 as much as other men ; but he believed that Germany would remain the stronger Power, that France needed an

outlet for her energies, that abstention involved abdica-
tion, and that she could only give hostages to fortune in
Africa and Asia if assured against attack from beyond
the Rhine. The fiery Déroulède, who founded his
Ligue des Patriotes in 1882, and who continued to pro-
claim that what had been lost by arms could only be
regained by arms, denounced the Premier as an atheist
of patriotism. 'You will end by making me think
you prefer Alsace-Lorraine to France,' rejoined Ferry.
'Must we hypnotise ourselves with the lost provinces,
and should we not take compensations elsewhere?'
'That is just the point,' retorted Déroulède. 'I have
lost two children, and you offer me twenty domestics.'
For the moment France was pleasurably excited by the
excursions and alarums of colonial adventure ; but the
forces represented by Déroulède and Clemenceau were
soon to change the political landscape

The year 1884 witnessed the foundation of Germany's
oversea empire and a sharp though transitory estrange-
ment between London and Berlin. Angered by the
evasive and procrastinating conduct of Lord Derby, our
Colonial Minister, Bismarck sought to win France for a
new plan. 'I wish to establish a sort of equilibrium on
the seas,' he declared to the French Ambassador on
September 23, 'and France has a leading *rôle* to play in
this connection if she will enter into our views. I do
not wish for war against England, but I wish her to
understand that if the navies of other nations unite they
will compel her to consider the interests of other people.
For that purpose she must accustom herself to the idea
that a Franco-German alliance is not an impossibility.'
Throughout the winter the Chancellor continued his
efforts to win over France. 'I hope to reach the point
when you will forgive Sedan as you have forgiven
Waterloo. Renounce the Rhine, and I will help you
to secure everywhere else the satisfactions you desire.'
He warmly eulogised the statesmanship of Ferry and
expressed the wish to meet him, perhaps in Belgium or
Luxemburg or even in the south of France. These

flattering advances made little impression on the new Ambassador in Berlin, Baron de Courcel. 'At bottom,' he reported, 'Bismarck wishes to do England a bad turn and to use us for the purpose.' On January 20, 1885, the sceptical Ambassador thus defines the schemes of the Wilhelmstrasse. 'To soften our memories, to turn our thoughts from the past to an indeterminate future and thus to lead us imperceptibly to swallow 1815 and 1871, so that France, accepting the hegemony of Prussia, henceforth gravitates in German orbits,—such is Bismarck's policy towards us. We must do him the justice to recognise the frankness and sincerity with which he declares it.'

Though Baron de Courcel had no intention of walking into Bismarck's parlour, some of his countrymen seemed prepared for the great surrender. 'You cannot think how much good our *rapprochement* has done,' observed Barrère, the French Minister in Cairo, to Herbert Bismarck. 'I cannot say there is no longer enmity, for that needs time, but there is no longer mistrust among us. It will still be a fairly long time till 1870 becomes merely a memory ; but only patience is needed for that. The *rapprochement* is not only the best for the two countries but for the world. We must think of future generations and remember that the strongest alliance would be France and Germany.' In the same month of September, 1884, General Campenon, Minister of War, entertained the foreign officers at the manœuvres at dinner, and observed to the chief of the German mission that the Government desired a *rapprochement* with Germany. 'A Franco-German alliance,' replied his guest, 'is only possible if you recognise the Treaty of Frankfurt.' 'That is what I am always telling my colleagues,' replied Campenon. 'We should no longer weakly occupy ourselves with the past, but should reckon with the present. With such an alliance France would at one blow regain her standing. France and Germany united would rule the world.' A fortnight later Herbert Bismarck visited Ferry, who charged him to tell the

Chancellor that he should not take the smallest step in Egypt without consulting the Wilhelmstrasse. ' We are on the high road,' remarked the Director of the Finance Ministry to Herbert Bismarck. ' First the *détente* and then the *entente*.' A few months after these flirtations a skirmish in the Far East shattered the dreams of reconciliation.

III

In the opening weeks of 1885 the news from Tonkin, which Ferry had added to the French colonial empire, became more and more alarming ; but on March 29 the Premier assured the Chamber that General Négrier possessed the forces needed to hold Lang-Son and to defend the frontier. On the following day a telegram announced that Négrier had been wounded and compelled to evacuate Lang-Son by superior forces. A wave of panic and fury, unknown since *l'année terrible*, swept over France. When the doomed Ministry demanded credits to retrieve the situation, Clemenceau sprang to his feet. ' We can enter into no discussion with you. We have no longer Ministers before us but men charged with high treason, on whom the hand of the law will descend, if the principles of justice still exist.' Ferry was hurled from power, peace was concluded with China, and the first period of colonial expansion of the Republic came to an abrupt end. The vote of March 30 was the condemnation not only of the greatest living French statesman but of the principle which had guided the policy of France since the Congress of Berlin. Gambetta and Ferry, with the encouragement of Bismarck, had sought compensation overseas for the loss of the provinces which, in their opinion, could not be regained within any measurable time. And now the glittering fabric of new-born empire seemed to crumble into dust. No more colonial adventures ! No more hazardous expeditions ! Ferry—*le traître, le Tonkinois*,—had forgotten the Vosges He had danced to Bismarck's piping and poured out blood and money in vain in the far places of the earth. *À bas le Prussien!* Back to continentalism! Back to the *Revanche*! It was the hour of Clemenceau.

The atmospheric change was reflected in the Ministerial declarations of the Brisson Cabinet. ' By a watchful and circumspect policy we must guarantee our position amidst the questions which pre-occupy Europe. The Republic desires nothing but peace, peace accompanied by the dignity which a nation like ours demands, peace assured by a solid army of defence.' The same *Leitmotif* was heard after the general election in the autumn. The first duty of the new Chamber, it was explained, was to strengthen the army. So powerful was the reaction that a demand for the total evacuation of Tonkin was only defeated by four votes in a crowded House. When Freycinet succeeded Brisson at the opening of 1886 his programme was fixed in advance by the imperious will of the electorate. ' If there is one point on which the ballot-boxes have expressed themselves without ambiguity,' ran the Ministerial Declaration, ' it is on the direction to be followed in foreign affairs. It is understood that France is to have a policy of dignity and peace, and that her forces are to be concentrated on the Continent, respected by all and menacing none. France desires no more of these distant expeditions, which are a source of sacrifice without any obvious compensation.'

The foreign policy of the Third Republic has been dominated by the two ideals of the recovery of the Rhine provinces and the foundation of an empire overseas. For the first two decades it seemed impossible to pursue them simultaneously, and it was equally impossible to found a colonial empire without the assent of Berlin. The first act ended when Gambetta and Grévy, Waddington and Ferry postponed the *Revanche* to the Greek Kalends and acted on the suggestion to take Tunis. The second act ended with the reverse in Indo-China, and the temporary abandonment of colonial expansion carried with it the termination of the Franco-German

détente. The two obvious tasks before France in her
new mood were to strengthen her army and to seek for
allies ; and the history of French policy during the
decade following the fall of Ferry is the record of her
successful pursuit of these objects.

Freycinet, who belonged to the school of Gambetta
and Ferry, desired to continue the friendly relations with
Berlin ; but he shewed less than his usual insight in
choosing a Minister of War whose sinister activities
were to bring France and Germany to the verge of war,
and to threaten the very existence of the Republic.
At this time, however, Boulanger was the *protégé* of
Clemenceau and the Radicals, and no one could foresee
coming events. The new Minister, who had seen service
in Algeria, Italy, Indo-China and the war of 1870, and
had served as Director of Infantry at the War Office and
commander of the army in Tunis, proceeded to justify
his selection by a series of reforms in the organisation
and munitioning of the army, the strengthening of fortifications, and the provision of creature comforts for the
poilu. Since the mind of France was at this moment
focussed on national defence, and since no comprehensive
reforms had been made in the army for a decade, he
quickly became a celebrity, and the facile acclamations of
the crowd aroused his political ambitions. Déroulède
offered him the services of the 300,000 members of the
Ligue des Patriotes. *La France Militaire, Le Drapeau,
La Frontière, L'Anti-Prussien, La Revanche,* and other
journals, old and new, sang his praises, announced that
France was ready, and preached the holy war.

' *Monsieur le Ministre de la Guerre,*' observed
Freycinet one day in July, 1886, ' *vous faites un peu
trop mon métier.*' The gentle rebuke produced no
effect, for the General relished his position on the crest
of the wave. People began to whisper and to watch.
It was not the German Embassy alone which began to
be alarmed. ' The topic of the day,' reported Lord
Lyons on July 2, ' is the conduct of Boulanger. He has
by degrees put creatures of his own into the great military

commands, and he is said to have used strange language in the Council of Ministers. From the way people talk one would think the question was whether he is aiming at being a Cromwell or a Monk.' A fortnight later Lord Newton, of the British Embassy, described his appearance at the fête of July 14. ' The mountebank had provided himself with a high-actioned black circus horse. As he pranced backwards and forwards and the public yelled their acclamations, President Grévy and the uninteresting crowd of bourgeois Ministers and Deputies seemed visibly to quiver and flinch. From that day Boulanger became a dangerous man.' The German Military Attaché sent home long reports on his activities and of the provocations of the press. ' The last few days have witnessed several remarkable outbreaks of chauvinism,' reported Count Münster, the German Ambassador, on October 14. ' The artificially stimulated hatred of Germany is if possible stronger than ever ; but the war of revenge is far from being popular. The wish that there may be one day a holy war is common to every Frenchman ; but the demand for its speedy fulfilment is met with a shake of the head.' Boulanger himself, added the Ambassador a few weeks later, was believed by some intimate friends to be afraid of war, since he knew too well the weak points of the army ; but he kept his fears to himself.

After a year's absence from Paris Prince Hohenlohe, the late German Ambassador, described in his diary on November 10, 1886, the new and alarming situation. ' What strikes me most is the change in Boulanger's position. In the spring of last year he was considered a *farceur*. Today he has the majority of the Chamber on his side. Freycinet does not dare to get rid of him, and even Ferry would find it difficult to form a Ministry without him. He knows how to win people and to dazzle the masses. If he stays two years longer in office, the conviction will become universal that he is the man to reconquer the provinces, and, as he is utterly unscrupulous and extremely ambitious, he will carry the masses into war. Blowitz agrees, and says that, if he remains, war will come in 1888. His fall is inevitable directly the country sees where he is leading it. Then he will be swept away, for the country is still pacific. But in a year it will be different.' ' In Boulanger,' echoed the Belgian Chargé a month later, ' the whole of France personifies her dreams of future greatness.'

During this orgy of chauvinism the French Government remained unmoved. The new Ambassador to Berlin, Herbette, who as Director of the Foreign Office had co-operated with Freycinet and enjoyed his confidence, arrived in October, 1886, and explained the views of his Government in a remarkable conversation with the Foreign Minister, Herbert Bismarck. The good services rendered by Germany in regard to France's colonial policy, he declared, were known only to the few. Now was the time to show the French people the real aims of German policy. ' What a *détente* there would be, and how all our suspicions and apprehensions would vanish if Prince Bismarck publicly declared that he would use his immense authority for the maintenance of the *status quo* in the Mediterranean ! All eyes would turn from the East, and we could employ all our resources in the Mediterranean, the theatre of our vital interests. It is a question of existence for us as a Great Power that England should evacuate Egypt. I assure you that the Mediterranean is the pivot of our policy and that the English are abominated in France, far more than the Germans have ever been. The idea of the *revanche* is out of date.' There was an element of unreality in such language when Boulanger was in the saddle, and it evoked no response in Berlin.

The reforms introduced or proposed by Freycinet and Boulanger, reducing the term of service from five years to three and improving the armament, challenged the superiority of the German army, and on November 25 the German Minister of War presented a seven year army bill increasing the troops by 41,000. ' It is only a question of time, measurable by years or half-years,' explained the *Kölnische Zeitung*, ' before the old struggle must be renewed.' The aged Moltke delivered a few oracular sentences. ' An *entente* with France has been mentioned. But while public opinion in France persists in demanding the restitution of two essentially German provinces, which Germany is firmly resolved not to cede, an *entente* is an impossibility.' The bill was fiercely contested ; but its supporters found their strongest argument in the growing popularity of Boulanger, who retained his portfolio when Goblet succeeded Freycinet in December. In the words of the new Premier, the whole of Europe was living ' on a footing of armed peace.'

On January 11, 1887, the Chancellor supported the Army Bill in one of the greatest of his speeches. Germany, he explained, belonged to what Metternich called satiated States ; but all the Powers were busy preparing for an uncertain future. ' Everyone asks, Is war coming ? I do not believe that any statesman will deliberately apply the match to the gunpowder heaped up in every land. But the passions of the mob, the ambition of party leaders, misguided public opinion—these are elements potentially stronger than the will of the rulers.' Germany had declined to thwart Russian ambitions in the Near East and had tried to oblige France everywhere except in Alsace-Lorraine. ' We have no intention and no reason to attack her. I would never fight because I thought a war might be inevitable. I cannot see into the cards of Providence. If the French will keep the peace till we attack, peace is assured for ever. Do we want more French soil ? I was not anxious to take Metz. I have complete confidence in the present French Government. Goblet and Flourens are not the men to make war. If you could guarantee their continuance in office, I would say, Save your money. But the stirring of the flames by an active minority makes me anxious. We have still to fear an attack—whether in ten days or ten years I cannot say. War is certain if France thinks she is stronger and can win. That is my unalterable conviction. Where is the Ministry who would dare to say, We accept the Treaty of Frankfurt? She is infinitely stronger than she was. If she won, she would bleed us white ; and if we won, after being attacked, we would do the same. There is also the possibility, even if France did not expect to win, that she might launch a war as a safety valve, as in 1870. Indeed, why should not Boulanger try it if he came to power?' On January 28 the Chancellor observed to Herbette that Boulanger's promotion to the Premiership or the Presidency would mean war almost immediately. On January 31 the *Post*, in an article entitled ' On the razor-edge,' which recalled the scare of 1875, argued that the retention of Boulanger in the Ministry was an imminent danger to peace.

The Reichstag accepted the proposed increase for three years instead of seven as demanded by the Bill, and the Government appealed to the country. The campaign was fought on the French peril. Boulanger, it was argued, was organising the *revanche*. Pictures appeared of the Vosges frontier with huge barracks and swarming *poilus* on the one side and not a soldier on the other. To ensure the desired response by emphasising the danger, the Government announced the calling up of reservists in Alsace-Lorraine. The atmosphere was electric, and war was anticipated by cool observers in other lands. On February 8 the French Chamber adopted without discussion Boulanger's demand for a special credit of eighty million francs, though the Cabinet vetoed his proposal for calling up reservists. Münster informally urged his dismissal, and the German semi-official journal observed that not a day had passed since his appointment to the Ministry of War without a measure to increase the offensive force of the French army. Once more, as in 1875, the Tsar was asked for and gave a promise of moral support. The German elections supplied the Government with the majority it needed, and the Army Bill became law in March.

With the passing of the Septennate there was a lull in the official German campaign against the French peril.

De Lesseps visited Berlin on a semi-official mission, and assured the Chancellor of the pacific disposition of the President and the Cabinet ; but so long as Boulanger remained a national hero, peace hung by a thread. 'Germany is making preparations for war,' reported Herbette on January 1, ' and opinion is being prepared for all eventualities. An imprudent word or manifestation might lead Bismarck to try to crush us.' At the end of April a spark seemed likely to set Europe ablaze. A French Police Commissioner named Schnaebele, an Alsatian who had opted for France in 1871, was invited by a German Police Commissioner to meet him for a discussion of administrative business. On reaching the rendezvous on the German side of the frontier he was seized, and after a struggle was carried off to Metz. The excuse for this gross outrage was that he had misused his official position to seduce German subjects to espionage, and that his arrest, if ever he crossed the frontier, had been decreed by the High Court at Leipsic. Once again Boulanger urged a military demonstration, and once more Grévy intervened to prevent it. Flourens kept his head, and forwarded to Berlin photographs of the letters of invitation from the German official. Bismarck at once admitted that the invitation implied a safe-conduct which must be respected. Within ten days of his arrest Schnaebele was at liberty, but was removed from his post. Though the Governments kept cool, the temperature of public opinion on both sides of the Rhine had risen to fever point. The fiery Déroulède taxed the Cabinet with cowardice, and argued that the time had come to finish with Bismarck's ' provocations.' Frenchmen maintained that Germany had tried to pick a quarrel, and Goblet, the Premier, declared that it would perhaps have been better to fight. The Germans continued to believe that Boulanger was master of France and might give the signal for invasion at any moment.

President Grévy, whose devotion to peace was only equalled by his contempt for Boulanger, had long

determined to get rid of the firebrand, who, as he subsequently confided to the German Ambassador, had on
two occasions proposed measures involving war. Goblet
resigned in May and Rouvier formed a Ministry without
the General, who was appointed to the command of an
Army Corps in the provinces. Both the President and
the Ambassador in Berlin argued that his influence had
been exaggerated and that the excitement had only been
on the surface ; but the danger was by no means at an
end. The mountebank remained the darling of the
crowd, and his ambition rose with his popularity. Every
missile aimed at him from beyond the Rhine served to
endear him to the Nationalists. When he was deprived
of his command in 1888 for paying visits to the capital
without leave, he stood for the Chamber at a by-election
in Paris as the champion of the revision of the Consti-
tution and was elected by an overwhelming majority.
Fortunately for the peace of the world, he was not built
in the heroic mould, and he let slip the opportunity
of marching on the Élysée to which his hot-blooded
followers summoned him. On learning that an order
had been signed for his arrest he fled to Brussels. The
bubble had burst. He was condemned in his absence
for treason, and a dangerous and discreditable career
was terminated by suicide. Boulanger, declares Freycinet, never really desired war ; but the Boulangist
movement had revealed the persistent vitality of the
revanche and rendered impossible a return to the *quasi-
entente* between Paris and Berlin.

The tension was once again reflected in the military
changes with which both Governments occupied themselves. In France the last remains of a professional
army were swept away, and every Frenchman on reaching
the age of twenty became subject to three years' service.
In 1888 Freycinet was appointed Minister of War,
and held the office for five years, carrying through the
three years' law, the development of the reserves and
the re-arming of the infantry. Germany replied by an
Army Bill reorganising the Landwehr and the Landsturm.

On February .6, 1888, in commending the Army Bill
to the Reichstag, Bismarck again surveyed the European
situation.   In 1887, he declared, the chief danger had
been from France ; now it was from Russia.   ' Since
last year one pacific President has succeeded another.
We can count on President Carnot to continue the
policy of M. Grévy.   We have also seen a change of
great importance in the Ministry.   The Ministers who
had a tendency to place their personal projects before
the peace of their own country and of Europe are gone,
and more peaceful men have taken their place.   I gladly
recognise that France is more pacific and less explosive
than last year.   Yet the danger of coalitions is permanent,
and we must arrange once for all to meet it.   We must
make greater exertions than other nations on account of
our position.   Russia and France can only be attacked
on one front ; but God has placed us beside the most
bellicose and restless of nations, the French, and He
has allowed bellicose tendencies to grow up in Russia.
I do not expect an early breach of the peace, but I advise
other countries to discontinue their menaces.   We
Germans fear God and nothing else in the world.'

IV

The fall of Bismarck in 1890 was hailed with delight
in France, and a slight *détente* began when the French
Government accepted the invitation of William II to
send a delegate to an international Conference on social
reform at Berlin.   The veteran statesman and publicist,
Jules Simon, who was chosen for the task, was captivated
by the charm, the frankness and the energy of his host.
The Kaiser expressed his ardent desire to enter into
cordial relations with France, and when his visitor
replied that the question could not be solved at present,
he rejoined that it was never too soon to formulate a good
idea.   ' Your army has made great progress and is
ready,' he added ; ' if it were engaged in single combat
with the German army no one could forecast the result

of the struggle. Therefore I should regard as a madman or a criminal whoever stirred up the two peoples to make war.' Jules Simon had no more doubt of the speaker's absolute sincerity than of the purity of his French accent. The diminution of tension was reflected in a slight mitigation of the rigid passport régime in Alsace-Lorraine.

In the milder atmosphere inaugurated by the visit of Jules Simon, the organisers of a picture exhibition in Berlin to be held in May, 1891, invited French artists to take part. The French Ambassador replied that his Government, though unable to participate officially in a private enterprise, would view with pleasure an acceptance of the invitation by French artists. This guarded reply was perhaps as much as Berlin expected, and invitations were now sent to individual artists in France. At a dinner at the French Embassy the Kaiser loudly expressed his admiration for French art, and eulogised with fervour the talent of Meissonier, who had recently passed away. Not content with verbal eulogies, he gave instructions for a letter in similar terms to be written to the French Ambassador, with the request to forward it to the Académie des Beaux-Arts. The French Government in return awarded to Helmholtz the medal of Grand Officier of the Legion of Honour, adding that this was the first time since the war that such a high distinction had been conferred on a German.

At this moment the French Ambassador was informed that the Empress Frederick was about to visit Paris incognito. Her object, it was explained, was to make purchases for her new home at Kronberg ; but she also desired to make the acquaintance of French artists and to induce them to exhibit at Berlin. In telegraphing the news Herbette added that the slightest *contretemps* might have disastrous results. The visit aroused the liveliest interest in both countries. Leading German papers described it as a historic event. ' Germany has given a fine example of her desire for reconciliation,' wrote the *Vossische Zeitung* ; ' will France respond ? May

we not hope that the chiefs of the French nation, in view
of the noble intentions of the Emperor's mother, will
abandon the ideas of revenge?' Such utterances
naturally provoked the Nationalists; and the ex-Empress,
who was never celebrated for tact, added fuel to the
flame by visiting the park of St Cloud and lunching
at Versailles. A protest meeting was addressed by
Déroulède, and several artists withdrew their acceptance
of the invitation to exhibit at Berlin. The German press
resented the protests and criticisms of Paris. 'The
French have not the right,' wrote the *Kölnische Zeitung*,
' to insult the august head of the German Empire and
his noble mother. Every German who has the slightest
sense of the dignity of his nation feels himself mortally
outraged in the person of his Emperor.' The Kaiser
was furious at the protest meeting, and the French
Government learned that measures preliminary to general
mobilisation had been ordered. The danger was obvious,
and the most careful precautions were taken to avoid
an incident at the departure of the ex-Empress, which
occurred an hour earlier than the advertised time. Not
till long after did the French people learn of the peril
thus narrowly averted.

On February 27, the day of her departure, Mar-
schall von Bieberstein, the Foreign Minister, addressed
Herbette in a tone which even Bismarck had never
adopted. After emphasising the good intentions of the
Empress, and stating that Berlin had expected a courteous
welcome and at any rate official protection against
insults, he added with calculated insolence : ' Clearly
one must not demand from a Republic what one would
from a strong government.' Even after making such
allowances, he explained, there were limits to tolerance,
and he hinted that they had been reached. The Ambassador, unaware that the Empress had already left
Paris, telegraphed in alarm that the slightest manifestation of disrespect to her might involve war. Thus the
visit which was designed to foster the *détente* inflicted
fresh wounds and revealed once again that the volcanic

fires were ready to burst forth at any moment. A few
days later the passport régime was restored in Alsace-
Lorraine in its full rigour. The countries had reverted
to the relations of 1887, but on this occasion there was
no Boulanger to hurl defiance across the Rhine. France,
moreover, had an additional reason to avert or at any
rate to postpone a conflict, for the Russian alliance, long
advocated by Boulanger, Déroulède and the Nationalists,
was in sight.

The conclusion of an alliance with Russia opens a
new chapter in the history of the Third Republic. If
the equilibrium which had been destroyed in 1870 was
not fully restored, there was at any rate no longer an
unchallenged German dictatorship in Europe. A few
far-seeing thinkers like Jaurès recognised that the
alliance might drag France into a war for Russian ambitions, and to fiery Nationalists it seemed to bring the
Revanche within the range of practical politics ; but
to France as a whole it symbolised complete recovery
from the disasters of 1870 and a guarantee against
menaces, humiliations and aggression. ' Now you are
two,' remarked Count Münster, the German Ambassador, to his friend Freycinet, ' you will find it difficult
to keep quiet. In France you are very thin-skinned,
and the slightest spark will set the powder alight.'
' What makes us sensitive,' replied the Minister of
War, ' is that we are thought to be weak. The stronger
we are, the less inclined shall we be to take offence.
Our relations will be easier when we stand on a footing
of equality. You will see that our *entente* with Russia
is a pledge of peace.' Feeling her flank secured, France
resumed her colonial ambitions after a lull of nearly a
decade. In 1894 Hanotaux entered on his memorable
term of office at the Quai d'Orsay. Like Gambetta and
Ferry, he believed that France would increase rather than
dissipate her resources by becoming a great colonial
Power. The only extensive field left for expansion was
in North and Central Africa ; but to push forward in these
vast regions involved friction and perhaps even conflict

with England. Thus once again colonial expansion involved a truce in the Franco-German conflict. The Kaiser renewed his attentions, and his telegram on the murder of President Carnot was particularly cordial. In 1894 France and Germany amicably arranged their frontiers in West Africa and combined to tear up a newly made Anglo-Congolese Treaty, while in the following year they co-operated with Russia in forcing Japan to disgorge Port Arthur.

In 1895 an invitation arrived from Berlin to send French ships to the opening of the Kiel Canal. The Cabinet desired to decline ; but when the Tsar formally urged France to join Russia in attending the ceremony, it consented on the understanding that the ceremony would be given no political significance. For once the Kaiser's speeches were tactful as well as eloquent. ' It is not only for our own national interests that we have worked. We open the gates of the canal to the peaceful intercourse of the nations. I welcome the participation of the Powers, whose representatives we see amongst us and whose magnificent ships we have admired, with all the greater satisfaction because I think I am right in inferring from it the complete appreciation of our endeavours, the very object of which is to maintain peace.' Despite his welcome to the French ships, however, he never conquered his contemptuous dislike of France and the French Republic. ' The Republicans are revolutionists *de natura*,' he wrote to the Tsar soon after the Kiel festivities. ' The blood of Their Majesties is still on that country. Has it since then ever been happy or quiet again ? Has it not staggered from bloodshed to bloodshed ? Nicky, take my word on it, the curse of God has stricken that people forever. We Christian Kings and Emperors have one holy duty imposed on us by Heaven, that is to uphold the principle of By the Grace of God. We can have good relations with the French but can never be *intime* with her ! '

A few months after the Kiel festivities the Jameson raid brought Great Britain and Germany to the verge of war. On January 1, 1896, the German Foreign Secretary visited the French Ambassador, and inquired whether France would join in ' limiting the insatiable appetite of England.' He did not propose co-operation in matters calculated to endanger peace, such as the Near East, Egypt or the Mediterranean, and he explained that there was no risk of an explosion ; but it was ' necessary to shew England that she could no longer take advantage of the Franco-German antagonism to seize whatever she wished.' Herbette replied that the exclusion of Egypt removed the principal reason which might induce France to join. ' I do not see what advantage such a league to hold England in check would be to us if we cannot count on your support in our interests.' Undeterred by this rebuff, the Kaiser despatched his fateful telegram to Kruger ; but the reaction of England was so menacing that he quickly retreated. A few weeks later, when France and Russia opposed the allocation of Egyptian moneys for the advance on Dongola, Germany supported the British request, and continued to flout French sentiment by steadily encouraging the reconquest of the Sudan.

Though Germany took the British side in the Egyptian quarrel, attempts were made at intervals by the Wilhelmstrasse to draw closer to France. In June, 1898, Bülow called the attention of the French Ambassador to *pourparlers* between England and Portugal, who, it was believed, was ready to give England a sort of mortgage on her colonies in return for financial aid, and to the danger of leaving London and Lisbon to settle their business without regard to the interests of France and Germany. On the following day the German Ambassador brought a Memorandum to the Quai d'Orsay suggesting economic reprisals against Portugal. The Méline Government had just resigned, and Hanotaux explained that he could merely hand it to his successor on his appointment. He himself regarded the Note as an invitation to a Colonial *entente* ; but Delcassé, the new Minister of Foreign Affairs, determined, before replying, to inquire if the complaints as to Portuguese action were justified. He learned that Portugal had no intention of alienating her rights, and accordingly sent no reply to Berlin. His omission even to acknowledge the German *démarche* illustrates the difference between him and his predecessor, and was followed by an Anglo-German treaty relating to the Portuguese colonies.

Undeterred by Delcassé's silence Berlin continued its approaches. The Kaiser, wrote the French Ambassador in February, 1899, was disposed to a *rapprochement* ; and the Naval Attaché at Berlin reported a conversation in which he expressed his pleasure at, the reception of German ships in Algiers and Tunis, and added that a French ship would be very well received at a German port. ' His Majesty is happy to see French public opinion better appreciating the real sentiments of Germany towards France, and he hopes that a real *entente* will soon be reached.' The Continent, he added, must unite in self defence especially against the dictation of England and America. A few days after the outbreak of the Boer war Bülow spoke to the French Ambassador of the identity of their interests in different parts of the world. ' In Africa you see that our interests are absolutely the same. Except the little triangle in regard to which we reached an arrangement with England last year, there is no point where we could not agree.' Delcassé replied that Bülow's opinion deserved to be examined in concert with Russia ; ' but I note that his conviction has never led the German Government to formulate any proposition.' When the French Ambassador now asked the Foreign Minister if he could explain how he conceived the reciprocal interests, he replied that he must have time to reflect. A few days after this curious reply, which would have been more relevant if the invitation to discussion had come from Paris, the Kaiser journeyed to England for the first time since the Kruger telegram, and Chamberlain, after conversation with Bülow, argued in his historic speech at Leicester

for an alliance or *entente* with Germany and the United
States.

The British reverses in South Africa at the close
of 1899 provoked plans of European mediation. On
February 28, 1900, Muravieff, the Russian Foreign
Minister, visited Paris and informed Delcassé that the
Russian Government wished to make the Wilhelmstrasse
declare itself by asking whether it did not think the time
had come for a joint *démarche* in London in the interest
of peace. Delcassé accepted the idea on condition that
the Russian Ambassador at Berlin spoke in the name of
Russia and France ; and he added that, if representations
were to be made to England, it was indispensable to
success that Germany should take the initiative. The
Russian Ambassador accordingly approached the German
Government. The Kaiser desired that Russia should
first inquire how a friendly intervention would be received in London, and added that, as it would be a long
business, the intervening Powers should first guarantee
each other's European territories for a certain time.
Since, however, even a temporary recognition of the
Treaty of Frankfurt was unthinkable for France, the
plan of joint mediation fell to the ground.

The Kaiser was probably not sorry to see the end of
the Russian project, and he continued his advances to
France, whose wrath during the Boer war was directed
against England. Germany patronised the Exhibition
of 1900, and in April, 1901, the French Government
accepted a pressing invitation to co-operate in the Bagdad
railway, on condition that Russia was admitted to the
enterprise ; but the consent of Russia, which regarded
the railway as an economic rival and a political danger,
was withheld. The conception of a Continental *bloc*,
consisting of Germany, Russia and France, continued to
haunt the Kaiser's brain, and the outbreak of the Japanese
war found Berlin and Paris in the same camp. What
more natural, argued the Kaiser, than that France should
enter a league which would guard Russia's flank during
the conflict and defend Europe against the maritime

and commercial domination of the Anglo-Saxons ? Thus the Treaty of Björko, after being discussed in 1904, was signed by the Kaiser and the Tsar in July, 1905. But the invitation to France to join was never officially made, since the treaty involved the mutual guarantee of frontiers. Even had the guarantee formed no part of the agreement, she would doubtless have declined to join an association directed against Great Britain, with whom she had by this time made up her quarrel.

V

The surrender of Fashoda led Delcassé, who had recently commenced his reign at the Quai d'Orsay, to seek compensation for Egypt in Morocco, and to gain from the friendship of England what he could not secure by thwarting her will. The *détente* began with King Edward's visit to Paris in the spring of 1903, and a year later the two countries sponged off the slate the main causes of friction. The attitude of official Germany towards the Anglo-French treaty was at first friendly. At Delcassé's reception on March 23, 1904, Prince Radolin asked if he might put ' an indiscreet question.' Was it true that an agreement had been or was about to be signed between France and England ? ' Neither one nor the other,' replied the Foreign Secretary ; ' but we have been conversing for some time with the London Cabinet with a view to the friendly settlement of the questions which interest our two countries. An understanding has been recognised to be possible, and will probably be reached.' ' Newfoundland is said to be in question ? ' ' We have spoken of it.' ' And Morocco ? ' ' Also. But you know our point of view on that subject. We wish to maintain the political and territorial *status quo* ; but if it is to last it must be improved. We have had to reinforce and increase our troops at considerable expense. The Sultan has experienced the value of our aid. It must be continued ; but it will be given in such a way that every one will derive advantage, since security is essential for commerce. Needless to add, commercial liberty will be strictly respected.' 'And Spain?' 'We shall respect her interests and legitimate aspirations.' Prince Radolin, added the Foreign Minister in recording the conversation, 'found my declarations very natural and perfectly reasonable.' On April 18, a fortnight after the treaties were signed, Delcassé instructed the French Ambassador to inform the Wilhelmstrasse that Lord Lansdowne and himself had been concerned exclusively with the interests of their own countries, without detriment to those of any other Power. He did not think it necessary to present a copy of the treaty, since it was already known to all the world.

Official comment in Germany was favourable. Germany, Bülow had declared in January, 1903, to the French Ambassador, had really no interests in Morocco, so insignificant were they at present. 'German commercial interests in Morocco are in no danger now,' wrote the *Norddeutsche Allgemeine Zeitung*, 'and greater stability would benefit us all.' 'We have no cause to imagine that the Treaty has a point against any other Power,' observed the Chancellor. 'It seems to be an attempt to remove a number of differences by peaceful methods. We have nothing, from the standpoint of German interests, to object to in that. As to Morocco, we are interested in the economic aspect. We have commercial interests, which we must and shall protect. We have, however, no ground to fear that they will be overlooked or infringed.' The Pan-Germans grumbled that Germany had been humiliated, and demanded the Atlantic coast; but the Kaiser informed King Edward at the Kiel regatta that Morocco had never interested him.

The despatch of the French envoy to Fez at the end of the year with a comprehensive programme of reforms was the signal for a change of front at Berlin. On February 11, 1905, the French Chargé at Tangier reported an ominous conversation with his German colleague. 'After the Anglo-French arrangement,' observed Kühlmann, ' we supposed the French Government was waiting for the Franco-Spanish agreement before putting us in possession of the new situation; but now that everything is settled we see that we have been systematically kept aloof. The Chancellor tells me that the German Government was ignorant of all the agreements concerning Morocco, and does not acknowledge himself to be bound by them in any way.' Delcassé instructed the French Ambassador at Berlin to complain of this language, and to remind the Government that he had answered Prince Radolin's inquiries on March 23, 1904 ; that, except Russia, Germany alone was informed of the Treaty before it was signed ; that no request for explanations had been made ; and that Berlin had also been informed of the Franco-Spanish treaty before it was published in September, 1904. The Under-Secretary, who received the complaint, replied that he knew nothing of Kühlmann's declarations, but added that Germany was not bound by the Anglo-French or Franco-Spanish agreements.

After the despatch of the French mission to Fez, Holstein, whose sinister influence was supreme in the Wilhelmstrasse, suggested that the Kaiser should visit Tangier. Bülow approved the plan, and the Kaiser reluctantly accepted their advice. The *Norddeutsche Allgemeine Zeitung* proclaimed that the French negotiations at Fez did not square with the avowed policy of maintaining the *status quo*. ' It is useless to attribute to the Tangier visit any selfish purposes against its integrity or independence,' declared the Chancellor in the Reichstag on March 29. ' No one who does not pursue an aggressive goal can find cause for apprehension. We have economic interests, and in Morocco, as in China, it is our interest to keep the open door.' Two days later the Kaiser landed at Tangier and addressed the German colony. ' The Empire has great and growing interests in Morocco. Commerce can only progress if all the Powers are considered to have equal rights under the sovereignty of the Sultan and respect the independence of the country. My visit is the recognition of this independence.' The theme was developed in a speech to the representative of the Sultan. 'It is to the Sultan in his capacity of independent sovereign that I pay my visit today. I hope that under his sovereignty a free Morocco will remain open to the peaceful competition of all nations, without monopoly or annexation, on a basis of absolute equality.' The Wilhelmstrasse took advantage of the collapse of Russia on the Manchurian battlefields to coerce her ally ; but this was not the main ground of its action. The French press had begun to speak of making Morocco a second Tunis, and Germany was convinced that, if she did not call a halt, Morocco would be swallowed up before her eyes. Her apprehensions were confirmed by the discovery that in addition to the published agreements of 1904, secret treaties of partition had been signed. The treaties were not published till 1911, but their provisions were quickly known at Berlin.

The charge against Delcassé of slighting Germany by not officially communicating the treaty of April 8, 1904, to the German Government is trivial ; but to a far graver indictment there is no reply. His fundamental error was in not purchasing in advance Germany's assent to French policy in Morocco. The good-will of Italy had been bought by recognition of her claims to Tripoli, that of Great Britain by assent to her position in Egypt, that of Spain by the hypothetical reversion of the Mediterranean coast. It has been argued that since Germany was not a Mediterranean Power there was no obligation to consult her. But she possessed treaty rights under the Madrid Convention of 1880 and under a separate commercial pact with Fez. Her trade was rapidly increasing and her readiness to take offence was notorious. Delcassé should have followed Ferry's example of securing the assent of Berlin before embarking on the conquest of Tunis. It was not only socialist critics like Jaurès who pointed out the dangers of his policy of neglect. 'By incredible blindness,' wrote René

Millet, an ex-Governor of Tunis, ' the Government took precautions with everybody except the only one of its neighbours whom it had serious cause to fear.'

Despite the provocation to which it was a reply, the Tangier demonstration proved a colossal blunder. French national feeling was aroused, and the limited obligation of diplomatic support involved in the Anglo-French treaty of 1904 developed into a general defensive understanding. German opinion was no less excited, and the impressionable Kaiser delivered a series of ominous speeches on the western frontier. ' I hope peace will not be broken,' he declared at Karlsruhe on April 27. ' I hope the events now in progress will keep the attention of our nation awake and strengthen its courage. I hope we shall find ourselves united if it becomes necessary to intervene in world politics.' Similar warnings were uttered at Mainz and Saarbrück. For the first time since 1891 the German sword began to rattle in its scabbard.

The Tangier warning was the first act of the Moroccan drama, of which the invitation to an international conference was the second. On April 11 Bülow, in a circular despatch, defined and defended his new policy. The Morocco treaty, he complained, was never communicated to the German Government ; yet Germany had not moved, since the treaty recognised the *status quo*, and he therefore assumed that France would consult the Powers if she aimed at changes limiting their rights. ' It was necessary to act when the Sultan asked us if France was in truth the mandatory of the Powers, when we learned of parts of the programme, and when great papers pointed to Tunis as a model.' A conference, he concluded, was the best solution, since Germany sought no privileges by separate agreement, and her interests were identical with those of other Powers. Meanwhile a German envoy had been despatched to Fez. A few days after his arrival in the Moorish capital the Sultan rejected the French proposals, and invited the signatories of the Treaty of 1880 to a conference at Tangier.

The invitation required an immediate reply, and Delcassé urged that it should be declined. The Foreign Minister had reigned at the Quai d'Orsay for seven years, and had been allowed a free hand in foreign affairs while the Dreyfus case was being liquidated and while Waldeck-Rousseau and Combes were wrestling with the Vatican. The Tangier demonstration, however, had at last compelled Ministers to lift their eyes from domestic controversies, and Rouvier, the Premier, held very definite ideas as to Franco-German relations. A disciple of Gambetta and an expert in international finance, he had no mind to allow France to be dragged into a struggle over Morocco. Prince Henckel von Donnersmarck was sent to Paris to explain the danger of the situation, and to urge the dismissal of the Foreign Minister. The air was thick with rumours of an ultimatum. At the decisive Cabinet, held on June 6, Delcassé argued that France could not go to a Conference without humiliation, that Germany was bluffing, and that he had just received the offer of an alliance from Great Britain, who would mobilise the fleet and land 100,000 men in Schleswig-Holstein. Rouvier, who took the German threats very seriously, replied that the Conference must be accepted. He was supported by all his colleagues, and the Foreign Minister, after warning them that their pusillanimity would encourage German insolence, withdrew and resigned. Rouvier's decision was inevitable ; for the Ministers of Defence confessed that France was unready for war, and the British offer of armed support was a legend.

On the fall of Delcassé Rouvier took over the Foreign Office, and explained to the German Government that he could only accept a Conference if a preliminary understanding on reforms were reached. 'If our proposals are accepted, all the Powers will benefit. We think a Conference dangerous without previous agreement and useless with it. But we do not definitely decline.' It would indeed have been dangerous to do so, as the French Ambassador at Berlin suggested after an alarming conversation with the Chancellor. ' He was very courteous, but he explained the necessity not to let this *question mauvaise, très mauvaise*, drag on, and not to linger on a road *bordé de précipices et même d'abîmes*. His insistence on an immediate decision struck me deeply and should influence your decisions. He added, however, that, if France accepted the Conference, German diplomacy would adopt an attitude which would satisfy us.' In part owing to the tactful mediation of President Roosevelt, to whom the Kaiser had appealed, Rouvier and the German Ambassador exchanged a Declaration on July 8 defining the conditions on which France accepted the Conference, and the Ambassador formally declared that France did not contest the Anglo-French agreement of 1904. A more detailed programme for the Conference was drawn up on September 28. The Conference was to be held at Algeciras, and both the French and German envoys were to leave Fez. At the end of the year Rouvier informed the Chamber of the agreement, adding that he looked forward with confidence to the Conference. At the same moment the Chancellor in the Reichstag defined his Moroccan policy as the preservation of economic equality in an independent state. Germany, he added, had a legal right to be consulted in any change in Morocco. ' The charge that we desire to attack France or to compel her to side with us against England is nonsense. I take full responsibility for the journey to Tangier, which Bebel calls the journey of provocation, but which was useful in bringing to general knowledge the international character of the question. *Cet animal est très méchant : quand on l'attaque il se défend.*' The situation was easier ; but the closer intimacy between Paris and London, dating from the Tangier demonstration, received a fresh extension at the opening of 1906 by conversations between Paul Cambon and Sir Edward Grey, and by the inauguration of secret discussions between French and British military experts.

Despite the preliminary agreements the Conference of Algeciras, which opened on January 16, 1906, was a prolonged battle between France and Germany, who received support from Austria alone. The main struggle arose on the control of the police in the ports ; and after a rupture had seemed in sight Germany reluctantly accepted a Franco-Spanish mandate under a Swiss Inspector-General. Bülow, on the other hand, established his contention that Morocco was the concern of all the Powers. The Rouvier Cabinet had fallen while the Conference was in session ; but Bourgeois, who followed him at the Quai d'Orsay, declared to the Chamber that the special rights and interests of France had been preserved. The Chancellor expressed no less gratification. Germany, he explained, had not desired to go to war on account of Morocco, where she had no direct political interests and no political aspirations ; but to prevent her treaty rights being disposed of without her consent was a question of prestige. The Chancellor's countrymen, however—and not the Pan-Germans alone—failed to share his satisfaction. He had a good hand, but he played it badly. He had recalled France from her absorption in domestic controversy to the unchanging realities of the Franco-German quarrel, and had stimulated French patriotic sentiment. But the most enduring result of the crisis, which lasted from the Kaiser's Tangier demonstration to the close of the Conference of Algeciras, was to tighten the bonds between Great Britain and France, to break down the barriers which separated Great Britain and Russia, and to prepare the way for the creation of the Triple Entente.

VI

It became the fashion after the first Morocco crisis to speak of *la nouvelle France* ; and there can be no doubt that the French nation emerged from the ordeal with a heightened self-confidence. ' Tangier,' writes the Abbé Ernest Dimnet in his interesting book *France Herself Again*, ' was a flash of lightning, after which the clouds lifted. What has been called the regeneration or even the resurrection of France dated from that shock.

Garrison towns like Toul, Lunéville, Verdun, and the lonely forts in their vicinity, the very names of which used to sound disagreeably in the ears of the recruits, became in great demand. The yearly manœuvres, which reservists had formerly been glad to shirk, were accepted as treats.' The moral support of Great Britain throughout the crisis strengthened the position of France as a Great Power. ' Henceforth,' writes Poincaré, ' we remained at least as closely united with her as with Russia. For several years the two Governments consulted one another day by day and hour by hour.' There was not a Premier or a Foreign Minister in the years immediately following the fall of Delcassé who thirsted for adventure ; yet there were elements in France, both old and new, to which the watchful waiting of official circles was pain and humiliation. The Nationalists damaged their cause at the time of the Dreyfus controversy by joining the enemies of the Republican régime, and in 1900 Déroulède was sentenced to ten years' banishment. He was allowed to return in the autumn of 1905, and the Ligue des Patriotes henceforth confined its energies to keeping alive the memories and ideals of the *Revanche*. The ideas which he represented received a powerful impetus from Charles Maurras, the founder of the new royalism in France. His scathing review of the foreign policy of the Republic, entitled *Kiel et Tangier*, appeared in 1905, and his *Enquête sur la Monarchie* in 1909. France, he declared, would never have a vigorous policy abroad or ordered progress at home without a King. In company with Léon Daudet he founded the journal *L'Action Française*, which gave the royalist cause a standing it had not possessed since the expulsion of the princes in 1886.

The poignant emotions of 1871 were also revived by two of the most accomplished French authors. The immense popularity of René Bazin's novel, *Les Oberlé*, published in 1901, and subsequently dramatised, revealed the undying interest felt by France in the fate of the lost provinces. The tragic cleavage of conviction and interest is mirrored in the fortunes of a single family living under the same roof. The grandfather, paralysed and speechless, but with the fires still burning hot within him, broods grimly over the scene like a figure in a Greek drama. The son, to whom the family business has been transferred, is guided exclusively by his interests, and has made his peace with the new régime. His daughter follows him willingly and his wife unwillingly ; but his son, Jean Oberlé, the hero of the tale, though he has been educated in Berlin and Munich and has never set foot in France, discovers on reaching manhood that, though he feels no hatred for Germans, his heart is French. He returns home to find the atmosphere poisoned by the undying feud. His desire to marry into a family of French sympathies is shipwrecked on the refusal of the parents to accept the son of a man who, in their belief, has been disloyal to France. After a few weeks of torment in his distracted home, where scenes are frequent and conversation impossible, Jean resolves to make his career in the fair country which he has never seen. The story ends with his desertion from Strassburg on the second day of his military service and a bold dash for the frontier, which he crosses with a bullet in his shoulder. His flight breaks off the engagement of his sister to a German officer, who declines to marry into the family of a deserter. Less tragic in character but no less popular are the novels in which Maurice Barrès, a Lorrainer and an ex-Boulangist, depicts the conflict of hearts and minds. *Au Service de l'Allemagne* describes the experience of Paul Ehrmann, a medical student at Strassburg, who, though French at heart, believes it his duty to remain in Alsace and hopes during his military service to make his comrades feel the moral superiority of France. *Colette Baudoche* portrays a girl in Metz who is asked in marriage, and asked in vain, by a German soldier whom she would gladly accept but for the impalpable barrier. Germany could boast of no novels or novelists to counterwork the subtle appeal of Bazin and Barrès.

In the lost provinces themselves time had wrought certain changes, but none of a fundamental character. The rapid development of industry increased the ties of interest with Germany, while the growth of socialism in the towns introduced a new line of cleavage. Moreover the breach between the French Republic and the Roman Church diminished the desire of good Catholics to escape from the German frying-pan into the anti-clerical fire. The old electoral struggle between the Autonomists and the *Protestataires* was in large measure replaced by the rivalry of Social Democracy and the Centrum. In 1911 the situation was eased by the grant of a Landtag and representation in the Bundesrath ; but the independence of the new body was not to the taste of the Government, and the Zabern incident shewed that the heart of the people had not been won, and that Germany was still in the iron grip of the military machine. Bethmann-Hollweg confesses and regrets that the Reichsland was regarded primarily as a military *glacis*. Forty years of German rule had brought unexampled material prosperity, but neither liberty nor contentment. The pictures of Zislin and Hansi were received with delight. Where France had succeeded in winning and keeping the sympathies of the inhabitants, Germany, with her heavy hand, conspicuously failed.

A further obstacle to Franco-German reconciliation was the Foreign Legion, in which men of different races who had made shipwreck of their lives sought oblivion or rehabilitation. To the new Germany, bursting with pride in her unity and her strength, it was an almost maddening thought that any of her sons should choose to enter the service and receive the pay of France, even under the burning African sun ; and it was universally believed that some of the renegades were seduced by French propaganda. The number of Germans serving at any moment was small ; but its mere existence was a perpetual irritant. It was a favourite theme of Pan-German agitators, and a special League of Defence against the Foreign Legion was founded at Munich.

VII

France did not allow the Act of Algeciras to thwart her designs in Morocco ; and in 1907, in consequence of local disturbances, she occupied Ujda on the Algerian frontier and Casablanca on the Atlantic coast. From 1906 to 1909, however, the rudder was in the hands of Clemenceau, whose dislike for colonial adventures was undiminished. In 1907 his Foreign Minister, Pichon, encouraged conversations between a French journalist and the German Legation at Tangier, which seemed to shew the possibility of a Moroccan Entente, based on the political *désintéressement* of Germany and an economic *condominium*. In January, 1908, Jules Cambon, the Ambassador at Berlin, reported that the Foreign Secretary desired to discuss an economic understanding. In March the Foreign Minister informed the Reichstag that Franco-German relations were normal and even friendly, and that Germany fully recognised the loyalty of France to the Act of Algeciras. These advances, however, were rudely interrupted by an incident which, like the Schnaebele crisis twenty years earlier, for some weeks threatened the peace of the world. Some German residents in Casablanca, aided by their Consul, had established an agency for organising desertions from the Foreign Legion, and in September, 1908, it persuaded two Germans, a German naturalised as a French citizen, a Russian, a Swiss and an Austrian to desert. The Consul provided them with civilian clothing, hid them in the city for some days, and resolved to embark them in a German steamer lying off the port. Early in the morning of September 25 they were accompanied to the harbour by a member of the Consulate ; but the boat in which they embarked capsized and they were forced to return to the shore. The Commandant of the harbour noticed them and gave orders for their arrest. A brief struggle ensued, and the German Consul vainly demanded the liberation of the three Germans.

Baron Lancken, Secretary to the German Embassy, appeared at the Quai d'Orsay and demanded ' prompt and complete satisfaction.' Pichon replied by demanding that the German Consul should be disavowed and censured. Neither side wished to fight, but the temperature rose rapidly. After a fortnight Germany proposed arbitration, which Pichon accepted. The Wilhelmstrasse, however, demanded the punishment of the port authorities at Casablanca and the release of the three German deserters, after which the German Consul would be punished. When Pichon rejoined that the matter was now referred to arbitration, the Ambassador again demanded the immediate liberation of the three Germans and compensation for two *employés* of the Consulate who had been injured in the scrimmage, and the Chancellor threatened to break off diplomatic relations. Pichon stood firm, and replied that he must await the arbitral award. The Chancellor now asked for an apology for the arrest of the deserters before the arbitration began. At this critical moment encouragements to stand fast arrived from London and Petrograd, and the Emperor Francis Joseph persuaded the Kaiser, who was staying with him, to settle the question amicably. The crisis ended as suddenly as it had begun. A declaration was signed by the two Governments regretting the events at Casablanca and referring questions of fact as well as of law to arbitration. The verdict of the Hague Tribunal, given some months later, censured ' the grave and manifest fault ' of the German Consulate in aiding the escape of the non-German legionaries, and added that the French authorities had acted correctly, except that needless violence had been displayed in the arrest of the deserters.

Though the two nations had once again looked war in the face, the discussion of an economic partnership in Morocco was quickly resumed. On February 8, 1909, Germany recognised the special political interests of France and promised not to oppose them, while France undertook not to thwart German commercial

and industrial interests. Both were to 'seek to associate
their nationals in the business which they may be able
to secure.' On the same day letters were exchanged
between Jules Cambon and Schön, the Foreign Minister,
declaring that the political *désintéressement* of Germany
did not affect the positions already held by her nationals,
but implied that they would not compete for posts in the
public services of a political character, and that when
their interests were associated it would be recognised
that French interests were the most important. The
agreement appeared to embody a profound modification
of Franco-German relations. Pichon declared that it
removed all causes of conflict in Morocco ; Prince
Radolin, the German Ambassador, observed that a
lasting *entente* had been secured, and the Chancellor
explained to the Reichstag that it assured France her
legitimate political influence without allowing her to
appropriate the country.

The pact of 1909 which raised such high hopes was
fated to be an apple of discord, for the good-will of the
Governments was paralysed by the incurable antagonism
of the peoples. The spoils to be divided consisted of
mines, public works and railways, and in all three so
many difficulties arose that at the opening of 1911 no
progress had been made. The question of railways was
complicated by the French claim to exclude strategic
lines from the *condominium* ; but an agreement was
within sight when in March, 1911, a change of Ministry
removed Pichon, the author of the pact of 1909, from the
Quai d'Orsay. His place was taken by Cruppi, who
desired to re-open the question. 'It would be very
inconvenient if we do not sign,' telegraphed Jules
Cambon from Berlin ; 'if we make Germany think that
we want to dodge the Convention of 1909, it would
create many difficulties.' But Cruppi, supported by his
colleagues in the Monis Cabinet, refused to sign without
further reflection. The unfavourable impression created
at Berlin was deepened by the simultaneous refusal of the
French Government to sanction a *consortium* arranged

between French capitalists in the French Congo and German capitalists in the Cameroons.

The decision of the Monis Cabinet to reconsider the railway agreement synchronised with rumours of a forward policy in Morocco, where civil war, tribal revolts and an empty exchequer had reduced the country to anarchy. On March 13, 1911, Kiderlen-Wächter, who had succeeded Schön as Foreign Minister, uttered a warning to Jules Cambon. 'German opinion might be excited, and it would be wise if Germany were informed in good time. By small successive operations France could be led on to an even more extended operation, which would end by annulling the Act of Algeciras.' The Ambassador replied that French plans were not fixed, but that the Act of Algeciras would be respected. On April 4 he intimated that France would probably be forced to occupy Rabat, and Kiderlen replied that he was apprehensive of the effect of the news on German opinion. On April 19 it was announced that in view of the danger to Europeans France had responded to the Sultan's appeal for aid by organising a column for the relief of Fez, which was surrounded by rebels, and that a French column would be available if required to succour the capital. Bethmann-Hollweg now added his warnings. Germany, he declared, had no reason to believe that the Europeans in Fez were in danger. 'You know German opinion on Morocco, and I must take it into account. If you go to Fez, you will stay there, and then the whole Moroccan question will be raised, which I wish at all costs to avoid. I do not say No, because I cannot assume responsibility for your compatriots; but I cannot encourage you. I can only counsel prudence.' 'The Chancellor,' reported Jules Cambon, 'does not seek adventures in Morocco and only wishes to maintain Germany's economic interests; not so the Pan-Germans. We must try to solve the problem without putting ourselves too much forward. I deplore the articles in our press on the Tunisification of Morocco, which are brought up against our official declarations.' The

German press began to peg out counter-claims, and even the *Berliner Tageblatt* clamoured for a port at Agadir. On May 1 the *Norddeutsche Allgemeine Zeitung* announced that a violation of the Act of Algeciras, voluntary or involuntary, would restore to all its signatories their liberty of action. Despite these reiterated warnings a French army marched to Fez, and rescued the Sultan from danger. The German view that a new situation had been created was shared by Spain, who proceeded to occupy the zone assigned to her by the secret treaty of 1904.

When the French troops had reached the Moorish capital, Cruppi attempted to reopen the railway negotiations. 'I am still very anxious about Morocco,' remarked the Chancellor to Cambon. 'German opinion is on the alert. French influence is growing, whether she wishes it or not. If you leave Fez, you will be compelled to return within a year. In Germany people will say that German interests are being neglected, and I see the possibility of extremely grave difficulties.' 'Possibly,' replied the Ambassador, 'but nobody can prevent Morocco falling one day under our influence. Why should we not discuss all outstanding matters except Alsace-Lorraine? We could try to give German opinion satisfactions which would allow it to watch our influence in Morocco develope without disquiet.' 'I will think it over,' rejoined the Chancellor; 'but go and see Kiderlen at Kissingen.'

On June 22 some very plain speaking took place at Kissingen. The situation, began the Foreign Secretary, had been completely transformed, with forces under French officers throughout the country and a Sultan at the orders of France. 'Have you forgotten the compact of 1909,' retorted the French Ambassador, 'which recognises French political influence?' 'Influence is not Protectorate,' rejoined Kiderlen; 'and you are on the road to organise a veritable Protectorate.' Cambon observed that it was not easy in dealing with a barbarous country to fix how far influence could go, and proposed

a general discussion like that between France and
England in 1903. ' I agree,' was the reply ; ' if we
confine ourselves to Morocco we shall not succeed.   It
is useless to plaster over a tottering structure.'   The
Ambassador explained that French opinion would not
allow Germany any part of Morocco, but ' one could
look elsewhere.'   ' Yes,' replied Kiderlen, ' but you must
tell us what you want.   Bring us back something from
Paris.'   Cambon travelled straight to Paris, where he
reported the conversation to Cruppi ; but the same
evening the Monis Cabinet fell and was succeeded by
Caillaux.   Before, however, the new Cabinet had time
to consider Cambon's communication, the German
Ambassador informed the Quai d'Orsay that a gunboat
had been sent to Agadir to defend German nationals
and interests.   The *Panther's* spring, like the Tangier
speech, ruined a good legal case.   Both countries had
repeated the mistake of 1905.   France pushed forward
in Morocco without disarming German hostility, and
Germany replied by banging her fist on the table.   Once
again Germany alienated the sympathies of the world,
and once again France found comfort and support in
her English friends.

On July 9 Jules Cambon and Kiderlen began the
conversations which were to continue for four months.
Germany, it was understood, would give France a free
hand in Morocco in return for compensation in the
Congo.   When, however, the Foreign Minister suggested the cession of the French Congo from the Sangha
to the sea, the French Government was alarmed, and
Mr Lloyd George intervened with the Mansion House
speech.   Kiderlen modified his demands, but he continued to ask more than France would consent to give ;
for German opinion was thoroughly aroused, and it was
not only Pan-Germans who demanded a slice of Morocco.
Early in September a financial panic in Berlin made the
Wilhelmstrasse more accommodating.   The Morocco
accord was signed on October 11 and the Congo treaty
on November 3.   The settlement was a triumph for

France, who rounded off her African Empire at the price of an unhealthy and undeveloped fragment of the tropics. The German Colonial Minister resigned in disgust. The Chancellor's statements that the *Panther* was not sent to acquire territory and that South Morocco was not a desirable possession for Germany were greeted with derisive laughter in the Reichstag. Kiderlen's threats of war and the outbursts in the Pan-German press added to the store of ill-will that had been accumulating in France for forty years, and strengthened the resolve to submit to no more humiliations. In Germany, on the other hand, the wrath of the people was directed far more against Great Britain for her intervention than against France for her stubborn defence of her interests.

VIII

The Agadir crisis was followed in England by a slight Anglo-German *rapprochement*, inaugurated by Lord Haldane's mission to Berlin, and in France by the accession to power of Poincaré. The personality of the new Premier made a deep impression on Izvolsky, the Russian Ambassador, whose recently published despatches vividly portray the revival of self-confidence in governing circles in France. During the twelve months of his premiership the bonds between the members of the Triple Entente were further tightened in view of the European war which few European statesmen expected to avoid. An Anglo-German neutrality agreement was frustrated, a Franco-Russian Naval Convention was signed, the French fleet was transferred to the Mediterranean, and the Grey-Cambon letters defined the relations between London and Paris. The belated blandishments of Berlin fell on deaf ears. When an agent of the German Foreign Office visited Paris in March, 1912, with the offer of ' wide autonomy in Alsace-Lorraine ' in his pocket, and entered into discussion with some prominent individuals, he found no response in the official world. ' The German Government,' commented Poincaré, ' seems to pursue with unwearying persistence a *rapprochement* which only a complete repudiation of the past would render possible. To listen to such propositions would be to quarrel with England and Russia and to lose the benefit of the policy which France has pursued for years. We should only obtain illusory satisfactions for Alsace, and we should find ourselves next day isolated.' Bethmann-Hollweg declares in his Memoirs that after the rise of Poincaré to power the French Ambassador in Berlin was a different man. He remained as courteous as ever, but the improvement of relations was no longer the theme of his conversation. The polite telegrams to the Kaiser which Poincaré quotes as evidence of the correctness of his attitude did not disguise the fact that the two nations had at no time since 1871 been further from a *rapprochement.*

The Balkan wars of 1912–1913 once more led Europe to the brink of the abyss ; but neither French nor German interests were directly involved. The ten months of conflict, however, left a deep and universal *malaise.* The German army, already slightly augmented in 1912 in consequence of the Morocco crisis, received in 1913 an increase of 170,000 men, the largest it had ever known ; and a capital levy of fifty millions was imposed to bring fortifications and artillery up to date. In introducing the Army Bill the Chancellor justified his demands by the displacement of power resulting from the Balkan wars, pointed to the growing menace of Pan-Slavism and French chauvinism, and spoke gravely of a conflict between the Teuton and the Slav. The Bill passed without opposition, for Germany was convinced that her safety could only be guaranteed by the strength of her own right arm. Austria was weakened by racial dissension, Italy an uncertain ally, Turkey defeated, and Roumania drifting towards Petrograd, while the enmity of France was unchanged, the hostility of Russia increasing, and the loyalty of Great Britain to her friends beyond reproach.

If Germany was conscious of her peril, she was also arrogantly conscious of her strength. Russia, it was widely believed, was rotten to the core, France decadent, England occupied with sport. In the middle of the nineties Bebel described his fellow-countrymen as still drunk with victory. Public opinion had grown ever more restless and excitable, and loudly insisted on Germany having her place in the sun. The centenary of 1813 increased the temptation to bluster and menace. ' The Kaiser is profoundly pacific,' wrote the Belgian Minister from Berlin on March 8, 1913, ' but the spirit of the governing classes is very different.' Though the Social Democrats emerged from the elections of 1912 the most powerful party in the Reichstag, the dangerous ferment among the middle and upper classes struck all observers. Otfried Nippold, returning after several years in the Far East, was shocked at the change, and in his *German Chauvinism*, published in 1913, courageously held the mirror up to his fellow-countrymen. Bernhardi's *Germany and the Next War* was only one of the books which proclaimed, as Treitschke had proclaimed to the previous generation, that war was part of the divine order. The Pan-German League, small in numbers but skilful in propaganda and insatiable in its demands, had been reinforced by the Deutscher Wehrverein, founded in 1912 by General Keim, who declared that a war was inevitable. The unwearying activities of Tirpitz and the Navy League found an eager response. ' There is a smell of blood in the air,' echoed General Liebert. The political Generals had become a national peril, but some of the journalists and professors were nearly as bad.[1] The peace-loving Bethmann-Hollweg sorrowfully confesses that Germany got on the nerves of the world.

The deeper aspects of the situation were reviewed at this moment in calm but grave tones in Prince Bülow's *Imperial Germany*. ' The resentment against Germany might well be called the soul of French

---

[1] See Vergnet, *La France en danger*, 1913.

policy. The other international questions are more of a material nature and only concern the body. It is a peculiarity of the French nation that they place spiritual above material needs. The irreconcilability of France is a fact that we must reckon with in our political calculations. It seems to me weakness to entertain the hope of a real and sincere reconciliation with France, so long as we have no intention of giving up Alsace-Lorraine. And there is no such intention in Germany. So long as France thinks she perceives a possibility of winning back the provinces, either by her own unaided efforts or with the help of others, so long will she consider the existing arrangement provisional and not final. The aim of French policy for many years to come will be to create the necessary conditions, which are lacking today, for a settlement with Germany with good prospect of success. It is a proof of a lively sense of honour if a nation suffers so keenly from a simple injury to its pride that the desire for retribution becomes the ruling passion of the people.'

Old friends and close observers began to detect a change in the Kaiser himself. ' He spoke with a note which was new to me,' reported Bishop Boyd Carpenter after a visit to Berlin in June, 1913. ' I felt that he was under the influence of a great fear.' ' From the beginning of 1913,' testifies Bethmann-Hollweg, ' he spoke to me of the coalition which was forming against us and would fall upon us.' His growing anxiety was revealed to King Albert at Potsdam in November, 1913. ' Enmity against us is increasing,' wrote the French Ambassador after the Belgian visit, ' and the Emperor has ceased to be the friend of peace. His personal influence has been exerted on many critical occasions, but he has come to think that war with France is inevitable. As he advances in years, the reactionary tendencies of the Court, and especially the impatience of the soldiers, obtain a greater hold over his mind. Perhaps he feels some slight jealousy of the popularity of his son, who flatters the passions of the Pan-Germans. The Emperor and his

Chief of the Staff may have wished to induce the King of the Belgians not to make any opposition in the event of a conflict between us. Whatever the object of the conversation, the revelation is one of extreme gravity. We must keep our powder dry.' In the following months Baron Beyens, the Belgian Minister, noticed that he was becoming less friendly to French visitors. ' I have often held out my hand to France,' he remarked at a Court ball in February, 1914, ' and she has replied with kicks. They had better take care at Paris, for I shall not always be here.' Colonel House, visiting Berlin in May, 1914, with a view to an Anglo-German-American Entente, was appalled by the militarism which surrounded the Kaiser. ' The whole of Germany is charged with electricity,' he reported. ' Everybody's nerves are tense. It only needs a spark to set the whole thing off.' Meanwhile a new series of incidents fanned the flame. When a Zeppelin descended at Lunéville, Frenchmen believed that it had come to spy ; and when some commercial travellers were molested at Nancy there was an outburst in the Reichstag, only partially appeased by the dismissal of the Prefect. Though the desire for war with France or anybody else was confined to a minute section of the German population, which did not include the Kaiser, the Chancellor or the Foreign Secretary, there was no general shrinking from a conflict and but little anxiety as to its result.

The atmosphere in France, though less neurotically excited, contained nevertheless explosive elements. ' The British attitude in 1911,' reported the Belgian Minister at Paris in October, 1912, ' caused a revulsion of feeling. To say that the French nation has become bellicose would be going too far. The agriculturist, the bourgeois, the merchant, the industrialist know what a conflagration would cost them ; yet the country is confident of success. We must count with the turbulent youth and the military. The men at the head of affairs are sincerely pacific, but their action is excessive. It is good to restore to a nation its dignity, but dangerous to

foster its chauvinism. They began by military parades
and marching through Paris. The visit of the Grand
Duke Nicholas excited nationalism. Millerand, the
Minister of War, accompanied him to the frontier,
whence the Grand Duchess saluted the lost provinces,
and the visit concluded with a review at Nancy which
became a demonstration against the Treaty of Frankfurt.
Opinion forced the hand of Napoleon in 1870, and could
again confront the Governments with a situation leaving
no issue but war.' The most chauvinist tirades in the
theatres and the *café chantants*, added the same witness
in May, 1913, aroused frenzied applause. Bencken-
dorff, the Russian Ambassador in London, reported his
impression that of all the Powers represented in the
Ambassadors' Conference France was the one who would
see war with the least regret. The election of Poincaré
to be President of the Republic in January, 1913,
proclaimed and increased the new spirit of confidence.
He remarked to the German Ambassador that the people
were pacific, but would not tolerate a second Agadir,
and his first act was to send Delcassé as Ambassador
to Petrograd to hasten the military measures agreed by
the General Staffs. The increase of the German army
compelled France to restore the three years' service
which had been discarded in 1905 ; and though the
law was strenuously fought by the Socialists and the
Caillaux Radicals, France, like Germany, was ready for
sacrifices.

The atmosphere of Paris during the last years of
peace is reflected in the thoughtful Memoirs of Schön,
who succeeded Prince Radolin at the Rue de Lille in
1910. The phrase ' friendly and neighbourly relations '
was used for the first time on his presentation to President
Fallières, and the new Ambassador did his utmost to
realise the ideal he had expressed ; but, like other
peacemakers, he found the path blocked by the impalpable
barrier. ' In spite of the lapse of forty years, in spite
of the country having achieved renewed prosperity, in
spite of the acquisition of colonial possessions, in spite

of having long since recovered the position of a Great Power, the wound of 1871 would not heal. The majority of the people were naturally less fierce with patriotic excitement as time went on ; but an active minority kept up the smouldering fire with a view to its bursting into flames at the given moment. When I suggested to M. Barthou, the Premier, that it was a great pity to exhaust ourselves on armaments and strife, he replied, ' *Rendez-nous l'Alsace-Lorraine, alors nous serons les meilleurs amis de la terre.*' In his lectures on the origins of the war Poincaré declares that France would never have taken the initiative in a war of liberation, and that no French Minister ever pronounced the word *Revanche* ; but he adds that they one and all declined to repudiate the two provinces and to be guilty of a cowardly betrayal.

The heads of the French army were no longer mortally afraid of their formidable neighbours. In a series of widely-read works, *La France victorieuse dans la Guerre de Demain*, *L'Offensive contre l'Allemagne*, and *L'Allemagne en Péril*, Colonel Boucher, ex-Chief of the Department of Military Operations of the General Staff, exhorted his countrymen to sleep quiet in their beds. France, it was true, was beaten in population, and was weakened by pacifism and ministerial instability. ' So Germany thinks she could defeat us, and treats us like a conquered country. But she is mistaken. This book proves that if we are attacked we are certain of victory. If war broke out tomorrow, we should certainly be supported by our two allies, Russia and England. We are sure of resisting till Russia invades Germany, and then we shall take the offensive and recover Alsace-Lorraine.' Another officer worked out the partition of Germany after the coming war.[1] During the two last years of peace the German Military Attaché in Paris sent home a stream of reports on the visible improvement of the French army.

In a remarkable volume, entitled *Faites un Roi, sinon*

[1] Lt.-Col. R. de D., *Le Partage de l'Allemagne. L'échéance de demain.*

faites la Paix, published in 1913, Marcel Sembat, an ornament of the Socialist party, implored his country-men to reflect and to choose. The system of alliances, he argued, was leading Europe towards war. The question of Alsace-Lorraine, he added, dominated the life and fortunes of France. It was necessary to decide between those who reluctantly acquiesced in the *status quo* and those who were determined on its overthrow at the first favourable opportunity. If the latter were adopted as the official policy, it was essential to restore the Monarchy and to concentrate every ounce of material and spiritual energy on preparing for the inevitable conflict. If, on the other hand, as the author, like Jaurès, desired, it was resolved no longer to challenge the verdict of Sedan, the quarrel should be brought to an end, all the more since, in his opinion, the population of the Rhine provinces dreaded nothing so much as war and wished for autonomy within the Empire. The author's countrymen rejected both the proffered alterna-tives of Monarchy and renunciation. Diplomatic and military preparations for the expected struggle were pushed forward. When the call from Petrograd came in 1914 France's unhesitating response was due not merely to her loyalty to the Russian alliance but to her hope that the sword of the Entente would restore the children she had lost in 1871 and had never ceased to mourn.

Two plain lessons emerge from the tragic story out-lined in this address. The first is that dictated settle-ments are apt to have short lives. The second is that the Franco-German feud, which began centuries before Bismarck and involves not only Alsace-Lorraine but the control of the Rhineland, is likely to continue till both nations, weary of their costly struggles, seek and find security and self-realisation in a world-wide League of Peace.